Uncle John's DID YOU KNOW...?

by the

Bathroom Readers' Institute

Bathroom Readers' Press
Ashland, Oregon

UNCLE JOHN'S
DID YOU KNOW...?
BATHROOM READER®
FOR KIDS ONLY

For information, write:
Bathroom Readers' Institute
P.O. Box 1117, Ashland, OR 97520
www.bathroomreader.com

Interior design/illustration and cover illustration:
Patrick Merrell
(*www.patrick.merrell.org*)

Cover design:
Michael Brunsfeld
(*Brunsfeldo@comcast.net*)

Uncle John's Did You Know...?
Bathroom Reader For Kids Only
by the Bathroom Readers' Institute

ISBN-10: 1-59223-682-0
ISBN-13: 978-1-59223-682-4
Library of Congress Control Number: 2006932283

Printed in Canada
Fourth printing November 2008
08 09 10 11 12 8 7 6 5 4

READERS' RAVES

Here's what our faithful fans have to say about Uncle John's Bathroom Readers.

"I love *Bathroom Readers*! They're interesting and funny. I can't stop reading them."

—Kevin

"I'm a teacher, and every morning I put a factoid from your books on the board. I have kids who can't wait to get to class to see what weird thing is on the board that day. You are a never-ending source of information and enjoyment. Thank you."

—Elly

"I have been a fan of the *Bathroom Reader* for over a decade now. Maybe one day there will be a whole course on bathroom reading, and quoting your text will not only be expected and encouraged, but required!!!"

—Jessica

"Your books are awesome!! ('Meow,' my cat agrees.) I have two books, *Uncle John's Top Secret Bathroom Reader For Kids Only* and *Uncle John's Puzzle Book*. Both of them have helped improve my grades by 20%!"

—Veronica

"I really love your *Bathroom Reader For Kids Only*. I'm 12, and I read it everywhere (not just in the bathroom!). I like it so much."

—Beka

THANK YOU!

The Bathroom Readers' Institute thanks those people whose help has made this book possible.

Gordon Javna
Amy Miller
Patrick Merrell
Stephanie Spadaccini
Angie Kern
Maggie McLaughlin
Brian Boone
Thom Little
Jay Newman
Julia Papps
Lorraine Bodger
Zackery Weimer
David Battino
Claudia Bauer
Michael Brunsfeld
Allen Orso
Connie Vazquez
Jennifer Thornton
John Dollison
Dan Schmitz
Judy Hadlock
Raincoast Books
Banta Book Group
Terri Dunkley
Sydney Stanley
JoAnn Padgett
Scarab Media
Steven Style Group
Jennifer P. & Melinda A.
Laurel, Mana, Dylan, and Chandra
Matthew Furber
Shobha Grace
Gideon and Sam
Porter the Wonder Dog
Thomas Crapper

*　*　*

While at sea, the crews of United States nuclear-powered submarines wear blue coveralls called "poopie-suits."

TABLE OF CONTENTS

DESTINATION: EARTH

JUST WEIRD

WORDPLAY

BELIEVE IT

BUILDING BIG

FILM, SCREEN & PAGES

IT'S HISTORY

FOOD FOR THOUGHT

ANIMAL ACTS

GOOD SPORTS

CUSTOMS AND FADS

FARAWAY FRIENDS

TAKE A NUMBER

ART & MUSIC

RANDOM FACTS

CREATURES SMALL

SCIENCE MADE FUN

AMERICANA

THE PEOPLE PAGES

HOW'S THE WEATHER?

GREETINGS FROM UNCLE KNOW-IT-ALL

Okay, nobody can know *everything*—not even Uncle John. But it's fun to know a little about a lot of different subjects. That's where your faithful friends at the Bathroom Readers' Institute come in. We love to collect fascinating facts and tantalizing trivia. Then we quiz each other: "Hey, Brian, did you know that you can hear an elephant's stomach rumble from 200 yards away?" Or, "Hey, Patrick, did you know that only 1% of the water on Earth is drinkable?" Or, "Hey, Stephanie, did you know that spiders sometimes get trapped in their own webs?" We could go on all day (and night) doing that, couldn't you?

Hey, what a great idea for a book!

So here it is: our kooky compendium of weird and wonderful facts—just like the encyclopedia...only fun. Use it to test your teachers, freak out your friends, mesmerize your mom, dazzle your dad, and baffle your brothers and sisters. (You may even feel yourself getting smarter.)

Happy reading and as always, *Go with the Flow!*

Uncle John and the Bathroom Reader Staff

MAN-MADE MILESTONES

• Hard hats were invented and first used in the building of the Hoover Dam in 1933.

• The sandals that the Statue of Liberty is wearing are size 879. (They're about 25 feet long.)

• The Great Wall of China stretches 1,500 miles and contains almost a billion bricks.

• On a clear day, you can see four states from the top of Chicago's Sears Tower: Illinois, Indiana, Wisconsin, and Michigan.

• The Eiffel Tower is repainted every seven years. It takes 60 tons of brown paint to do the job.

• There's evidence that after the Pilgrim ship *Mayflower* sailed from England to America (and back), it was taken apart and made into a barn in England.

• What kind of stone is Mount Rushmore made of? Granite. It was "carved" mostly with dynamite.

• Egypt's Great Sphinx is 260 feet long, 20 feet wide, and 65 feet tall, making it the largest stone statue in the world.

• While the rest of the world had wheels, the Aztecs had no knowledge of them.

12

ENGLISH

Even if you speak it, there's still plenty to learn about it.

• There are only three words in English that use "en" to pluralize them: ox (oxen), brother (brethren), and child (children).

• While many Western languages, such as Spanish, Italian, and French, are Latin-based, English isn't—it's mostly derived from German.

• There are 812 three-letter words in current usage in the English language, and 857 fifteen-letter words.

• The Brooklyn accent—saying "dese, dem, and dose" for "these, them, and those"—came from the Dutch accent of the original settlers. Want to hear a Brooklyn accent? Just listen to Bugs Bunny.

• In 1737 Benjamin Franklin made a list of American slang terms for drunkenness—and came up with 228 of them.

• "Pants" was a dirty word in England in the 1880s.

• "Dreamt" is the only English word that ends in the letters "mt."

• The North American National Scrabble Association recognizes five words worth 392 points—the most anyone can score in a single turn: OXAZEPAM, BEZIQUES, CAZIQUES, MEZQUITS, and MEZQUITE.

ALL ABOUT EARTH

Some of the things you could tell a visiting Martian about your home planet.

• Lake Baikal in Russia is the world's deepest lake—it's deep enough for five Empire State Buildings to stand in it on top of each other.

• Millions of years ago, the Earth consisted of one land mass surrounded by a vast ocean. Geologists call the land *Pangaea* (Greek for "all land"); they call the ocean *Panthalassa* ("all sea").

• Sometime between 180 and 200 million years ago, Pangaea broke into two parts: *Laurasia*, which consisted of what is now North America, Europe, and part of Asia; and *Gondwanaland*—what's now South America, Africa, Australia, India, and Antarctica.

• Where's the Earth's core? Directly under your feet, 4,000 miles down.

• Tallest mountain on Earth: Not Mt. Everest—it's Hawaii's Mauna Kea, which rises 33,476 feet from the floor of the Pacific Ocean.

• Want to travel as fast as a jet plane while standing still? Stand on the equator. The Earth's spin is greatest there, moving you at more than 1,000 miles per hour.

• What do you call the tip of a glacier? The *snout.*

• The way at which the Earth is tipped on its axis—at an angle of 23½°—is what causes the seasons.

• Scientists think the Earth's core is hotter than the surface of the Sun.

• Take a deep breath: If air were liquid, it would form a layer over the Earth about 33 feet deep.

• Wind blowing against a mountain range can actually speed up or slow down the Earth's rotation.

• California's San Andreas fault is slipping about two inches a year, causing Los Angeles to move closer to San Francisco. At this rate, L.A. will be a San Francisco suburb in about 15 million years.

• 95% of all life on Earth lives in the range between 300 feet below sea level and 9,000 feet above sea level.

• It hardly moves, but it accounts for 85% of all life on Earth: It's plankton, which consists of microscopic plants and animals that float around in the water.

• About 100 million tons of sand particles travel around the Earth every year, carried by breezes.

• Here comes the tide: The Atlantic Ocean is getting wider by an inch or more every year.

• In the last 10,000 years, Niagara Falls has moved about 10 miles upstream. That means that the falls are eroding at the rate of five feet a year.

• What's the most abundant element in the Earth's crust? Oxygen. (Second most abundant: silicon.)

EVERY 24 HOURS...

...without fail, here's what happens...

- The Earth travels more than 1.5 million miles in its orbit around the Sun.
- 2.5 billion adults go to work; 1 billion kids go to school.
- Lightning strikes 8 million times.
- The bees of the world make 3,300 tons of honey.
- Crayola makes 5 million crayons.
- The world's humans produce 2.2 billion tons of poop.
- 200,000 Americans have surgery.
- Two people in Sri Lanka die from poisonous snakebites.
- Birthdays are celebrated by 16.5 million people.
- Americans eat 15 million hamburgers.
- The chickens of the world lay 2 billion eggs.
- The Amazon River gushes 8 trillion gallons of water into the Atlantic Ocean.
- 380,000 babies are born; 145,000 people die.

IT'S ANCIENT HISTORY

• Ancient Celtic warriors were known to fight naked. From head to toe, their skin was dyed blue.

• The Arabs didn't invent Arabic numerals—the Hindus of India did. The numerals were introduced to Europe by way of Arab traders around the 11th century.

• The Romans used IIII to represent the number 4, as opposed to IV, because IV was the symbol reserved for Jupiter, the chief Roman god.

• The first recorded wrestling match took place in Japan in 23 B.C.

• The city of London was founded in 43 B.C.

• The longest Roman aqueduct was 87 miles long. It's still there—in Tunisia—but it's been falling into ruin since the 14th century.

• No one knows exactly what Cleopatra looked like, but she was probably not nearly as beautiful as she's depicted in the movies.

• King Hammurabi's code of laws was carved into a eight-foot-high stone that was placed in the middle of Babylon 3,700 years ago—even though hardly anyone at the time could read. If you ever want to see it, it's in the Louvre Museum in Paris.

GAMES

• Historians think the game of darts originated as archery practice for soldiers.

• Chinese checkers was invented in Germany.

• In 1991 Judit Polgar of Hungary, age 15, became the youngest chess Grandmaster in history. Her sisters, Susan and Sofia, are also chess champions.

• Some soda vending machines in Japan have a game built in. If you press the drink-selection button at the right moment, your drink will be free.

• Charades was so popular in the 1930s and 1940s that it was called "The Game."

• Jacks is descended from a game called "knucklebones" that was played with sheep bones.

• The average speed of a dart heading toward a dartboard is 40 mph.

• Playing tip: You can extend a game of Hangman by giving the hanging man a hat, bowtie, and shoes.

• The game Othello originated in China more than 3,000 years ago, but in Japan it was a favorite game of the samurai.

• Croquet made its first and last appearance at the Olympics in 1900. The matches also marked the first time that women competed in the Games.

AMAZING ANIMALS

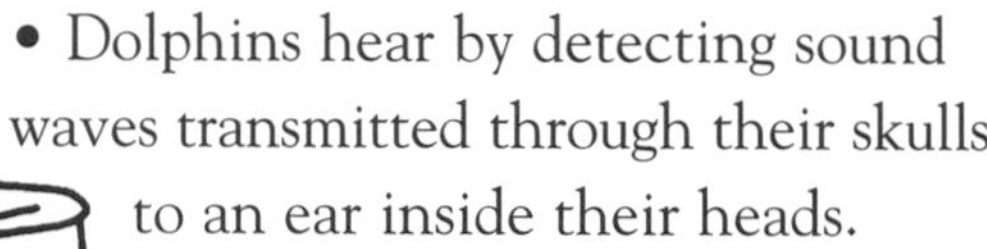

• Dolphins hear by detecting sound waves transmitted through their skulls to an ear inside their heads.

• Hippos can drink as much as 66 gallons of water per day.

• A hungry polar bear can smell a seal from 20 miles away.

• Like dogs and wolves, rhinoceroses mark their territory by urinating.

• The honey badger's favorite food? Honey, of course. To get to this prize, they'll withstand hundreds of bee stings, an assault that would kill almost any other animal.

• One female mouse can give birth to more than 100 babies during a year.

• A platypus carries half of its body fat in its tail…and can draw on this energy reserve when food is scarce.

• The toucan must turn its head backward and rest its bill on its back to sleep.

• Three overcoats were once found in the stomach of a single shark.

JAPANESE SAYINGS

• Ever laugh so hard you busted a gut? The Japanese expression for a belly laugh is "to boil tea with your belly button."

• No matter how talented you are, sometimes you still don't succeed. That's why the Japanese say "even the monkey falls from the tree."

• Even if you think you're hiding, others can often still see you. The Japanese call that "hiding your head and showing your butt."

• When bad things seem to pile up, we say, "When it rains, it pours." The Japanese say, "The bee stings while you're already crying."

• A very popular person in Japan is called a "pulled octopus." It's like everyone is tugging on a different tentacle.

• If you're a big fish in a small pond, you may believe you're better than you really are. The Japanese say, "A frog in a well doesn't know the ocean."

• The English expression "casting pearls before swine" means giving something valuable to someone who won't appreciate it. The Japanese call it "giving a coin to a cat."

FREAKS OF NATURE

- Slugs have four noses.
- A praying mantis has only one ear.
- Not only do honeybees have hair on their eyes, they also have five eyes: three small ones on the top of their heads and two bigger ones in front.
- Snails have been known to sleep for three years. (No wonder it takes them so long to get anywhere.)
- A chameleon can move its two eyes in different directions at the same time.
- The boto dolphin of South America is unique among dolphins. Why? It's pink.
- Open wide: Small birds called plovers are the dental hygienists of the animal world. They'll hop into a crocodile's open mouth and clean its teeth.
- The pupil of an octopus's eye is rectangular.
- Armadillo moms always have four babies at a time. And the babies are always all the same sex.
- Freakiest freak? Here's our candidate: The horned lizard uses special muscles to burst tiny blood vessels at the edges of its eyes so it can squirt a stream of blood at an attacker—from as far as three feet away.

CARS BY THE NUMBERS

Hop in and take this baby for a spin!

• The average American-made car contains 300 pounds of plastic.

• Why do they call it "rush" hour? In London rush-hour traffic moves at—ho-hum—just eight miles per hour.

• Eww! Roll down the windows! Over a lifetime, the average driver passes 912 pints of gas inside a car.

• In 1990 there was a traffic jam 84 miles long in Japan—a world record.

• Can you guess how long it took to assemble one Model T Ford on a production line in the 1920s? Answer: 1 ½ hours.

• In 1900 there were 109 automobile companies worldwide. Today there are about 2,000.

• About one man in three admits to daydreaming while driving.

• The six stars on the Subaru logo represent the Pleiades, a star cluster in the constellation Taurus.

• The average driver will honk 15,250 times in a lifetime. (Most American cars honk in the key of *F*.)

• You could have bought a Model T Ford for $260 in 1925.

• About half the German highway system has no speed limit.

• The average driver will curse 32,025 times in a lifetime of driving.

• The average person will spend two weeks of their life waiting for traffic lights to change.

• Early cars didn't have steering wheels—they used levers.

ONCE UPON A TIME

In which we present a few stories about stories you may have read as a child.

• Even though seeing a mermaid on a ship voyage was considered bad luck, the statue of Hans Christian Anderson's Little Mermaid in Copenhagen harbor attracts a lot of sailors who touch her for *good* luck.

• The Brothers Grimm didn't write those fairy tales; most were folk tales not meant for children. The brothers collected them from storytellers and began publishing them in 1812.

• Ever heard of Charles Perrault? Maybe not, but you know the 17th century Frenchman for his Mother Goose stories, including Cinderella, Puss-in-Boots, Little Red Riding Hood, and Sleeping Beauty.

• In the original folk tale, Goldilocks wasn't a little girl who ate the bears' porridge. She was an old woman who drank the bears' milk. (In another version, she wasn't even Goldilocks—she was Silverhair.)

• What's Little Red Riding Hood's first name? It's not "Little"...it's Blanchette.

• Oh, no, an ogre! The name Shrek comes from the German word *schreck*, which means "fear" or "terror."

LAST NAMES

The origins of some common American last names that were based on old-time occupations.

• A "Carter" was a delivery person who drove a cart from town to town.

• If your name is Cooper, one of your ancestors might have been a maker of wooden barrels. (From the old Dutch word *kupe*, meaning "tub.")

• The name Kellogg literally means a hog-killer, a nickname for pork butchers, derived from "kill hog."

• A "Parker" wasn't a parking valet, he was the grounds-keeper of a park surrounding a nobleman's estate.

• The name Stone comes from a worker who cut stone for a living.

• In the Middle Ages, "Leach" was a word for "doctor." It came from an old English word *laece*, that also meant "leech"—because medieval doctors used blood-sucking leeches on their patients.

• A "Black" was a cloth-dyer whose specialty was shades of black.

• Do you know anyone named Chamberlain? A chamberlain was a personal servant who cleaned the chambers (rooms) of a nobleman's home.

• A "Kemp" was a wrestler—from *cempa*, the old English word for "champion" or "warrior."

THE COLD TRUTH

• At 3° to 10°F, snowflakes are usually star-shaped. When it gets a little warmer, they're shaped more like columns; a little colder, more like plates.

• Home Sweet Home: A Canadian company offers a two-day course in igloo building.

• Brazil, 2003: A 440-pound chunk of ice fell out of a cloudless sky. Scientists blamed it on global warming.

• Here's how fast an average raindrop falls: 600 feet per minute. The average snowflake falls at a more leisurely pace: about 11 feet per minute.

• Record for the most snowfall on a single day: 47.5 inches of snow fell on Valdez, Alaska, on January 16, 1990.

• Look out below! A snowflake that spins like a top as it's falling will usually be symmetrical when it hits the ground; if it falls sideways, it will probably be lopsided when it lands.

• Dirty snow melts faster than clean snow. Why? Because dirt particles are warmer than snow crystals.

IT'S A WILD WORLD

• Mountain goats have a special feature on each hoof: a soft pad that acts as a powerful suction cup. Result: A mountain goat can walk up very steep mountains.

• The detergent most commonly used to clean elephants is Murphy's Oil Soap.

• The housefly hums in the key of *F*.

• Why can't birds live on the space station? Because they require gravity to swallow.

• What do reindeer and chimpanzees have in common? They both like bananas.

• Koalas' fingerprints are nearly identical to humans'. (They could actually be confused at a crime scene.)

• The world's termites outweigh the world's humans 10 to 1.

• A full-grown eagle is powerful enough to kill a young deer and fly away with it.

• Some species of snails are venomous and can kill an adult human with a single bite.

• Wolverines, the largest members of the weasel family, have been known to pry apart the jaws of a steel trap they've been caught in.

OH, CANADA

• Canada has roughly 2 million lakes...more than half the lakes in the world.

• The last Canadian dollar bill was issued in 1989. It was replaced by the one-dollar coin, commonly called a "loonie"—after the loon bird engraved on it.

• St. Paul, Alberta, is home to the world's first flying-saucer launching pad. It was built in 1967 to celebrate Canada's centennial.

• Room to roam: On average, there are nine people per square mile in Canada, as compared to the 76 people crowded into each square mile in the U.S.

• The Dutch Royal Family moved to Ottawa as refugees during World War II. In gratitude, Princess Juliana of the Netherlands gave Ottawa 100,000 tulip bulbs in 1945.

• North America's largest shopping mall: the West Edmonton Mall in Alberta. In addition to over 800 stores and restaurants, it boasts an amusement park, an indoor lake with four working submarines, 26 movie theaters, and a hockey arena.

• Canada and the United States share the longest unbroken boundary in the world—nearly 4,000 miles.

• Unusual Canadian place names: Blow Me Down, Spuzzum, Head-Smashed-In Buffalo Jump, and Ta Ta Creek.

SWEET DREAMS

• Good news for people who are lactose intolerant: Chocolate aids in digesting milk.

• Now *that's* progress: The first lollipop machines made 40 lollipops a minute. But today's rate is 5,900 lollipops a minute—nearly 100 per second.

• The secret to blowing bigger bubbles is to chew your gum until the sugar is gone; sugar makes bubbles collapse because it doesn't stretch.

• Candies that have been around for more than 100 years: Hershey bars, Tootsie Rolls, Cracker Jack, Good & Plenty.

• More than half of the marshmallows sold in summer are toasted over a fire.

• The world's largest S'more was made from 20,000 toasted marshmallows and 7,000 chocolate bars. It weighed 1,600 pounds.

• The world's largest lollipop (including the stick, of course, or it wouldn't be a lollipop) weighed 4,031 pounds, measured 18.9 inches thick, and was more than 15 feet tall. The flavor was cherry.

• Imagine a plastic Easter egg about the height of a nine-story building. That's how big it would have to be if it was filled with the more than 16 billion jelly beans that U.S. manufacturers produce for Easter every year.

ADVENTURES IN BUBBLE-LAND

• Part 1: Coat the inside of a glass with vegetable oil and then pour in some soda pop. You won't see many bubbles yet. That's because the oil smooths over the microscopic bumps (called *nucleation sites*) that draw the carbon dioxide gas out of the soda.

• Part 2: Now, drop some sugar into the soda and...bubbles galore! The rough surface of the sugar crystals provides the nucleation sites necessary to extract the dissolved gas.

• Part 3: Where does all that foam come from in an ice cream float? Answer: The rough, icy surface of the ice cream draws the bubbles out of the soda, and then milk proteins coat the bubbles, producing a sturdy foam.

• Part 4: Mixing baking soda (a base) and vinegar (an acid) is another way to make carbon dioxide bubbles.

• The Grand Finale: Outside, in as big a space as you can find, open a large bottle of diet soda and position it so it won't tip over. Warn any spectators to stand a few feet back, then drop a whole roll of Mentos candies into the bottle at the same time, and get out of the way. The soda will erupt like a fireworks display.

ARTSY-FARTSY

- In 1983 Japanese artist Tadahiko Ogawa made a copy of the *Mona Lisa* completely out of toast.
- Van Gogh signed his paintings using only his first name: Vincent.
- Frederic William Goudy designed 122 different typefaces. (You're reading one of them right now.)
- Leonardo da Vinci never put a signature or date on the *Mona Lisa.*
- German artist Bernd Eilts fashions dried cow manure into wall clocks and small sculptures.
- Van Gogh's *Portrait of Dr. Gachet* sold for $82.5 million, making it the most expensive painting ever sold at auction. It now belongs to a private collection.
- Artist Claes Oldenburg created a 45-foot-tall clothespin for Philadelphia's Centre Square Plaza. (Shouldn't it be in *Wash*-ington?)
- In 1940 four French teenagers found a cave with wall paintings that dated back to the Upper Paleolithic Era—between 30,000 and 10,000 B.C.

- In a 2004 poll to find "The Greatest Dutch Person," Rembrandt and Van Gogh came in 8th and 9th respectively—right behind Anne Frank.

THE SEVEN WONDERS OF THE ANCIENT WORLD

• **The Great Pyramid** is the oldest wonder, and the only one still standing. It was built as a tomb for Pharaoh Khufu, probably in 2680 B.C. It is made of 2,300,000 blocks of stone—the average weight of each block is 2.5 tons.

• **The Hanging Gardens of Babylon.** Persian king Nebuchadnezzar II built the gardens for his wife in 600 B.C. in what is now Iraq. On top of 75-foot-tall columns were terraces covered with trees, flowering plants, fountains, pools, and mechanical waterfalls.

• **The Statue of Zeus at Olympia.** The Greeks built this 40-foot-high statue of gold, jewels, and ivory to impress visitors to the ancient Olympics. Built in A.D. 450, it was destroyed in a fire in A.D. 462.

• **The Temple of Artemis** at Ephesus, Turkey, was built in 550 B.C. to honor the goddess of the hunt. It was destroyed in 356 B.C., then rebuilt—and then destroyed again in A.D. 262. Some of its columns survived and are now in the British Museum in London.

• **The Mausoleum at Halicarnassus** was erected in Bodium, Turkey, by Queen Artemisia in memory of her husband, King Mausolus, who died in 353 B.C. All that's left of it today is the foundation, some statues (in the British Museum), and the word "mausoleum," which has come to mean a large aboveground tomb.

• **The Colossus at Rhodes** was a 105-foot-tall bronze statue of the sun god Helios, overlooking the harbor of the Greek island of Rhodes. Completed in 280 B.C., it was destroyed during an earthquake around 224 B.C. Though no one knows exactly what the statue looked like, some historians think Helios wore the same headdress as the Statue of Liberty.

• **The Pharos of Alexandria** was a working lighthouse for 1,500 years until it was destroyed by an earthquake in the 14th century A.D. It was about 400 feet tall, the height of a 40-story skyscraper. Some deep-sea divers think they've found the ruins of the lighthouse, and there are plans to reconstruct it.

ON SAFARI

• When Europeans first saw these tall animals, they thought they were a cross between the spotted leopard and the camel, so they called them...*cameleopards*. We call them giraffes.

• Reebok named their shoe brand after a type of African gazelle.

• Do ostriches really bury their heads in the sand? No. They do lower their heads to fight, and will lower their heads and necks to hide...but only if they're sitting on a nest.

• A lion's mane protects him during fights with other lions.

• A hyena is one of the few animals that will attack a lion.

• What's gnu? The name "gnu" is from a West African language that pronounced the "g." (We don't.) The word probably came from the gruntlike sound that gnus make.

• Female lions do most of the hunting. Its the males' job to defend the herd (called a "pride") against intruders.

GLUG GLUG

Water, water everywhere.

• About 72% of the Earth's surface is underwater.

• The Seven Seas: Antarctic, Arctic, North Atlantic, South Atlantic, Indian, North Pacific, South Pacific.

• Every minute that your kitchen faucet is on, it pours out about three gallons of water.

• You use about two gallons of water to brush your teeth if you leave the water running.

• The longest freshwater shoreline in the world is located in the state of Michigan.

• The United States is 27 times larger than Norway, but Norway has a longer coastline. Why? Because of Norway's *fjords*—deep inlets with steep cliffs, the longest of which reaches 127 miles inland.

• There are more than a million swimming pools in Florida...even though no one in Florida lives more than an hour's drive from the ocean.

• Average depths: The Java Sea is 151 feet deep; the Arctic Ocean is 3,407 feet.

• The Pacific Ocean is about 12 times larger than the Arctic Ocean.

HAPPY HOLIDAZE

• "Rollo, the Red-Nosed Reindeer"? Almost. That was one name author Robert May considered before he decided on Rudolph. (Reginald was another.)

• Early Easter baskets were made to look like birds' nests, with eggs and other treats tucked inside.

• What workers receive the most Valentine's Day cards? Teachers, of course.

• Under the rule of Emperor Claudius, the Romans had 159 holidays per year—that's one almost every other day. (Whoopee!)

• Who buys greeting cards? Women, mostly—they purchase a whopping 93% of all cards sold.

• 54% of New Year's resolutions are broken within two weeks.

• When's Easter? Good question. It's celebrated on the first Sunday *after* the first full moon *after* the first day of spring. With this complicated formula, there are 35 dates in March and April on which it can fall.

• In Finland, Santa rides on a goat named Ukko.

• How fast does Santa's sleigh have to go to deliver a gift to every kid in the world on Christmas? Over two million miles per hour.

THAT'S DISGUSTING!

- Scabs are nature's Band-Aids: They start to form less than 10 seconds after you get cut, and they keep germs out while the cells underneath make new skin.
- Your mouth is one of the most crowded parts of your whole body: More than 100,000,000 micro-creatures are in residence there at any one time.
- London's parks are watered by more than a million gallons of dog urine every single year.
- 50% of women and 90% of men do not wash their hands after they've used the bathroom…unless someone is watching them.
- Think your kitchen sponge is clean? Wrong! It contains more bacteria than your toilet.
- Amateur biologist Ruth Nauss was a true lover of slime mold: She kept specimens (she called them "pets") in jars and took them along with her on vacation. One slimy pet lived for more than nine years.
- When a wasp attacks a skipper caterpillar, the little wormlike critter fires defensive poop balls from its butt. These missiles travel at six feet per second! Evidently the smell of skipper caterpillar poop is like perfume to the wasp, because it will turn around and immediately zoom off in the direction of the dookie.

LOONY LAWSUITS

Think the classroom's weird? Try the courtroom.

• Actual court case: *The United States v. 350 Cartons of Canned Sardines.*

• Shades of Stephen King: A 375-pound woman stepped on a 53-year-old grave, and it collapsed under her weight. She's suing the cemetery.

• *Harry Potter* publisher Scholastic sued a newspaper for more than $100 million for running a review of Harry's latest book three days before it was released, and revealing the surprise ending.

• Someone is suing Palm, Inc. for "deceptive marketing practices" because one of their PDAs was advertised as displaying more than 65,000 colors—but it's really only capable of producing 58,621.

• A 15-year-old boy who joined a Babe Ruth Baseball League didn't get to play as much as he thought he should. He sued the league for a refund of his entry fee. (He lost.)

• A lot of junk: A man who was having heart attacks and got diabetes because he's obese is suing McDonald's, Burger King, Wendy's, and KFC because they didn't tell him that he shouldn't eat so much fast food.

HERE, DOGGIE

• Top dog: When two dogs approach each other, the dog that's wagging its tail very slowly will be the dominant of the twosome.

• Detector dogs trained to look for drugs at airports can sniff out 400 to 500 packages in about 30 minutes.

• Every pile of dog poop that goes unscooped attracts about 144 flies.

• For every 130 dogs who try out for police work, only one is qualified.

• It may look like one, but according to breed standards, it isn't officially a Chihuahua if it weighs more than six pounds.

• Bloodhounds aren't specialists in smelling blood—their name comes from "blooded hound," referring to their pure breeding.

• A group of greyhounds is called a *leash* of greyhounds.

• The Basenji is known as a dog that doesn't bark. That's a myth—it does bark on rare occasions. But it sounds more like a scream.

• Those little dogs called "lapdogs" were once popular among the wealthy because they could be put into bed first to attract the bedbugs and fleas. (Eww!)

• Newfoundlands are good swimmers because they have webbed feet.

AROUND THE WORLD

• Next to Warsaw (the largest city in Poland), there are more people of Polish origin in Chicago than in any other city on Earth.

• About 85 million people live in deserts. That's about 13% of the world's population.

• The South Pacific nation of Fiji is made up of 332 islands, most of which are uninhabited.

• The official dance of Mexico: the Mexican Hat Dance.

• The Yanco tribe of the Amazon cannot count beyond three. Why? They don't have any words for larger numbers.

• There are 75 towns in the world named Waterloo.

• Most rivers flow south, and a few flow north, but the Tonle River in Cambodia does both. Six months of the year it flows north, and the other six months it flows south.

• Lost and Found Department: In one year, 7,026 umbrellas and 19,583 articles of clothing were found on London's buses, trains, and taxis.

THE ANCIENT OLYMPICS

• The first event at the first Olympics, held in 776 B.C., was a foot race. The winner was Koroibos, who worked as a cook.

• The Games were held every four years for 12 centuries—until A.D. 393.

• The ancient Olympic Games never had a marathon race. The first marathon was held in Athens in 1896.

• Famous Greeks like Socrates, Plato, Aristotle, and Hippocrates attended—or even competed in—the ancient Olympics.

• In A.D. 67, the Roman emperor Nero won a series of events—not because he was a great athlete, but because he was the emperor of the most powerful state in the world and everybody had to lose to him.

• No holds barred: The *pankration* event was a kick-boxing and wrestling match between two men. It could go on all day, and everything was allowed except eye gouging, nose gouging, biting, or using a weapon.

• According to ancient Olympic regulations, bribing a judge or an opponent would be punished by whipping.

• Married women weren't allowed to attend the ancient Games. If they were caught, they'd be thrown off a cliff.

EVERYBODY'S BODY

• The human body is mostly water—about 70%. How watery are you? If you weight 80 pounds, 56 pounds of it is water. That's about 112 eight-ounce glasses of water in *you*.

• Every day about 10 billion tiny scales of skin rub off your body.

• The Japanese believe blood types determine personality traits. Type A: calm, trustworthy. Type B: creative, excitable. Type AB: thoughtful, emotional. Type O: confident, good leader. (Uncle John is Type O.)

• Itch, ouch, itch, ouch: Babies who wear disposable diapers are five times more likely to get diaper rash than babies who wear cloth diapers.

• Sweaty feet? No wonder! Feet have about 250,000 pores oozing a quarter of a cup of liquid each day.

• A blink lasts about .15 seconds. Every person blinks for roughly 23 minutes per day. In just one day, all the blinks of all the people in the world would add up to 267,000 years of darkness.

• Mom is right: Carrots *are* good for your eyes. Your body converts the carotene in carrots into vitamin A, which is essential for proper vision.

GEOGRAPHICAL RECORDS

• Brazil has the most plant species in the world: more than 56,000.

• Not the grandest? The deepest canyon in the United States isn't the Grand Canyon. Hell's Canyon, along the Oregon-Idaho border, is more than 8,000 feet deep. The Grand Canyon is less than 6,000.

• World's largest city: Davao City, in the Philippines, with an area of over 1,500 square miles.

• China is bordered by more countries than any other: Its 16 neighbors are Afghanistan, Bhutan, India, Kazakhstan, Kyrgyzstan, Laos, Macau, Mongolia, Myanmar, Nepal, North Korea, Uzbekistan, Pakistan, Russia, Tajikistan, and Vietnam.

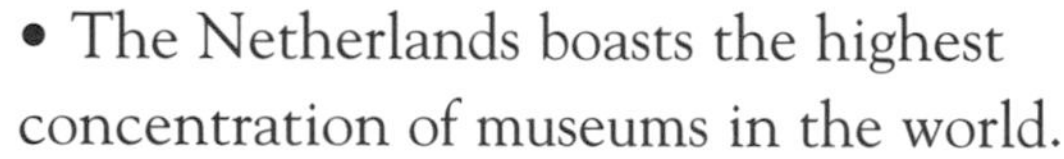

• The Netherlands boasts the highest concentration of museums in the world.

• Ushuaia, Argentina, is the southernmost city in the world.

• Hawaii's Mount Waialeale is the world's wettest location: it gets about 460 inches of rain per year.

• The steepest street in the world is Baldwin Street in Dunedin, New Zealand, with an incline of 38%.

INSTRUMENTAL

A little background music, please, maestro…

• Instruments named after their inventors: the saxophone (Adolphe Sax), the Moog synthesizer (Dr. Robert Moog), and the theremin (Leon Theremin). The sousaphone was named after bandleader John Philip Sousa, but he didn't invent it.

• After some California preschool students took musical keyboard lessons for eight months, their IQs rose by 46%.

• In 2006 a violin made in 1707 by famed violin maker Antonio Stradivari sold for $3.5 million.

• Some scientists believe that Stradivarius violins sound so good because of microscopic holes in their wood. The holes may have come from soaking the wood in seawater or coating it with borax.

• Former president Bill Clinton played the saxophone in jazz bands when he was a teenager.

• The combined tension of the strings in a grand piano is as much as 30 tons.

• Traditional circus music was played on a calliope (ca-LIE-oh-pee), a kind of organ that runs on steam. It was named for Calliope, the Greek muse of poetry.

• *Ukulele* is Hawaiian for "jumping flea," because a player's fingers move really fast when playing it.

44

WORLD RELIGIONS

• The first religion to spread beyond the society where it originated: Buddhism.

• Medieval experts on religion believed there were 399,902,004 angels in the universe.

• There's a statue of Buddha in Tokyo that's 394 feet tall—more than twice the height of the Statue of Liberty.

• Seven out of 10 people believe in life after death.

• The ancient Egyptians worshiped more than 2,000 different gods and goddesses.

• According to Norse mythology, Valhalla, the heaven reserved for brave Viking warriors slain in battle, has doors so wide that 800 warriors could walk through them shoulder-to-shoulder.

• But I couldn't help it! The Puritans considered being born on a Sunday a huge sin.

• Some people think the Shroud of Turin bears Jesus Christ's image at his crucifixion. Others think it's a hoax, possibly perpetrated by Leonardo da Vinci.

• Hinduism is one of the world's oldest religions, dating to 1500 B.C. Hindus call their religion *sanatana dharma*, meaning "eternal truth."

ANIMAL DEFENSES

• To save their colony, some ants can actually explode in the face of the enemy.

• Some lizards have tails that break off when grabbed by an attacker. The lizard slips away, leaving the attacker holding the tail. (Not to worry, though: The tails do grow back.)

• Ready, aim, fire: The spitting cobra spits its venom right into the eyes of its enemy.

• Skunks aren't the only animals that rely on bad odors to repel their enemies. Bedbugs, cockroaches, earwigs, foxes, minks, snakes, weasels, and wolverines do, too.

• The jawfish spits pebbles at attackers.

• Playing possum: Most people think that when opossums are threatened they pretend to be dead. Turns out they don't—they actually faint from sheer terror.

• Zebras defend themselves with their hooves and teeth. What about their stripes? It's possible that the stripes of a fast-moving herd make it hard for a predator to focus on any one animal.

• Among North American snakes, the eastern hognose has the most elaborate defense behavior: When threatened, it flattens its head and neck like a cobra and hisses loudly. Then it may strike, though it rarely bites. If these ploys fail, the snake rolls over, writhes as if in pain, opens its mouth, sticks out its tongue, and plays dead.

• Fence lizards defend themselves with camouflage: They look like tree bark, especially when they remain perfectly still.

• The slo-o-o-w-moving sloth uses camouflage as its main defense: It will hide beneath branches or curl into a ball in the fork of a tree to resemble a termite nest or a knot in the wood.

• Fake-out: The scarlet king snake (which is not venomous) looks similar to the deadly eastern coral snake. So any predator that fears the coral is very unlikely to attack the scarlet.

• Electric eels, electric catfish, and electric rays all live up to their names: They emit an electrical shock to stun or injure attackers.

• The skin of a skink (a type of lizard) is covered with scales that overlap smoothly, making them slippery and difficult for predators to catch.

VOLCANOES

• Since the beginning of recorded history, about 550 different volcanoes have erupted on the surface of the Earth—but a lot more than that have erupted on the ocean floor.

• The word "volcano" probably comes from Vulcano, a volcanic island near Sicily, Italy. The island's name came from Vulcan, the god of fire in Roman mythology.

• What countries have the most active volcanoes? Indonesia, Japan, and the United States, in that order.

• Mount Kilauea (kee-la-WAY-ah) on the island of Hawaii is the most active volcano on Earth. Perhaps that's because it's the legendary home of the powerful—and short-tempered—goddess Pele (peh-LAY).

• Fifty American volcanoes have erupted in recorded history.

• The Yellowstone Caldera (a caldera is the crater of a volcano) in Yellowstone National Park is at least two million years old. It hasn't erupted violently for the last 640,000 years.

• While lava is still underground, it's called *magma*.

• Hot lava eventually solidifies to form two kinds of lava, both with Hawaiian names. One is *a'a* (AH-ah), whose surface is rough and broken; the other is called *pahoehoe* (pah-HOY-HOY) and has a smooth surface.

WHADAYA SAY?

Italians say "pronto" *when they answer the phone, meaning "I'm ready." Here are some more facts about other languages.*

• Schools in different parts of India teach courses in 58 different languages.

• The word *ka* has 214 different meanings in Japanese.

• Only 19% of the people in Wales can speak their nation's historic (and co-official) language, Welsh.

• The Sanskrit word for "war" means "desire for more cows."

• The letter F can be pronounced five different ways in Icelandic.

• In Brazil the number six has two different names: *seis* and *meia*. Because *seis* and *três* (three) sound similar, Brazilians say *meia* (which means "half," as in "half-dozen") when saying phone numbers.

• There are 6,800 languages in the world, but experts think half will be extinct by the end of this century.

• Only one person in the world still speaks the Eyak language: Marie Smith, of Anchorage, Alaska—and she's 88 years old.

• Nearly 900 million people in the world speak Chinese; 341 million speak English. How many American schoolchildren study Chinese? About 50,000.

MAKE A WISH

• Why do we throw coins in fountains to make wishes come true? The ancient Greeks started it—they threw coins in their wells, hoping to keep the wells from running dry.

• The first wishbones were used by the Etruscans, who lived 2,500 years ago in what's now Italy. They would lay the wishbone in the sun to let it dry, and people would come by to stroke it and make a wish.

• A wishbone is a turkey's clavicle, or collarbone.

• The things that a bride wears for good luck: something old, something new, something borrowed, something blue. The tradition comes from a poem, the next line of which is "and a silver sixpence in her shoe."

• When an eyelash falls out, put it on your finger, make a wish, and blow it away.

• Next time you find a penny, wear it in your left shoe and your wish will come true.

• People wish on a falling stars, rainbows, a new moon, or the first star they see at night.

• A sure way to make a wish come true is to kiss your elbow. Go ahead, try it!

• In medieval England, mincemeat pie was a common Christmas dish. People believed if you made a wish on your first bite of pie, it would come true.

ALPHABET SOUP

• If the English alphabet were lined up in the order from the most frequently used letters to the least used, it would look like this: E T A I S O N H R D L U C M F W Y P G V B K J Q X Z.

• Q is the only letter in the alphabet that does not appear in the names of any of the 50 United States.

• Longest entry in Webster's dictionary: the word "set," with 75 definitions.

• The only 15-letter word that can be spelled without repeating a letter is "uncopyrightable."

• The longest place name in the world is *Taumata-whakatangihangakoauauotamateaturipukakapikimaunga-horonukupokaiwhenuakitanatahu*, in New Zealand. In Maori it means: "The brow of the hill where Tamatea—the man with the big knees, who slid down, climbed up and swallowed mountains, traveled the land and is known as the Land Eater—played his nose flute to his loved one."

• A *tilde* (~) over an n in Spanish changes the sound from "n" to "nya." So *mañana* is pronounced "mah-NYAH-nah."

• You'd think the last letter of the Greek alphabet should be zeta, but it's not—it's omega.

LOST & FOUND

• Certain species of mice build "signposts" out of leaves and twigs to keep themselves from getting lost.

• In 2001 archaeologists in Syria found a 3,800-year-old recipe for beer.

• It is estimated that, on average, one of the world's languages disappears every two weeks.

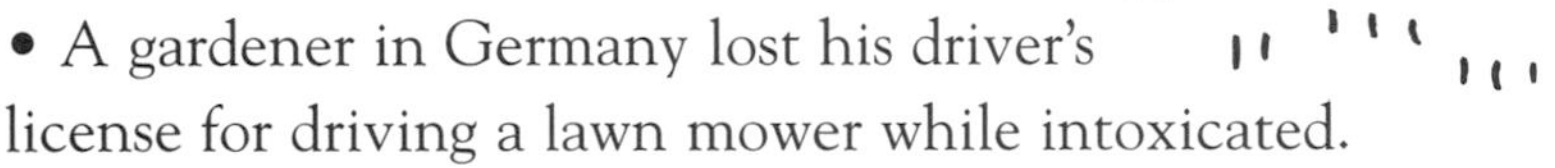

• A gardener in Germany lost his driver's license for driving a lawn mower while intoxicated.

• Some of the items found during California's annual Coastal Cleanup Day: two phone booths, a styrofoam Tiki god, Scooby-Doo underwear, a plastic eyeball, a "Just Married" sign, half a bowling ball, fuzzy dice, a check written to Taco Bell for $8.78, Dracula teeth, and porcupine bones.

• Mountain climber George Mallory—who, when asked why he wanted to climb Mount Everest, uttered the famous line "Because it is there"—disappeared on the mountain in 1924. His body was recovered in 1999 at 21,300 feet.

• In 2005 the most valuable buried treasure in history was found on an island off the coast of Chile. The booty, buried by pirates in 1715, included gold and jewels now worth more than $10 billion.

WORD-OLOGY

Bat around some big words and show everybody how smart you are.

- The study of ants is called *myrmecology*.
- Compulsive nose picking is called *rhinotillexomania*.
- *Scatologists* are scientists who study poop. When most people use the word "scatological," they mean obscene.
- A flea expert is a *pullicologist*.
- Vomiting is also called *emesis*, from the Greek word for puking.
- Snap your fingers. That's called a *fillip*.
- The last word in many English dictionaries is *zyzzyva*, the name of a tropical weevil. It's also sometimes used to mean "the last word" in any situation.
- If you've never had a haircut, that makes you *acersecomic*.
- Sounds like a fun job: People who study laughter are called *gelotologists*.
- *Taphephobia* is the fear of being buried alive.
- *Plutology* is the study of wealth. A plutocrat is a wealthy person.
- *Mammonism* is the greedy pursuit of riches, "mammon" being the biblical word for material wealth.

FOOD & DRINK

• Think pizza: America's best-selling herb is oregano.

• Americans eat 75% of their raisins at breakfast.

• The world's longest sushi roll measured 328 feet in length.

• The most valuable lunchbox in the world? A 1954 Superman lunchbox that sold for $13,500 at auction.

• The Incas used to create highly prized pots in the shape of peanuts.

• There are five basic flavors: sweet, sour, salty, bitter, and *umami*—the savory taste of meat.

• No one knows how 7UP got its name.

• Gelatin, an important ingredient in Jell-O, marshmallows, and Gummy Bears, is made from cow (or pig) bones, hooves, and connective tissues.

• Iodine is added to salt because most people don't get enough iodine in their diet. Lack of it can lead to a goiter, a swelling of the thyroid gland (on the neck).

• Germany's 1,300 breweries produce more than 5,000 varieties of beer.

• Three billion people eat rice as the main staple in their diets.

• The coffee crop is so important to Colombia's economy—they're the second largest producer of coffee after Brazil—that every car that enters the country is sprayed for bacteria that might damage the crop.

• About half the processed food in grocery stores contains genetically modified ingredients.

• The clementine, a cross between a tangerine and a sour orange, was an accidental hybrid said to have been discovered by, and named for, Father Clement Rodier in the garden of his orphanage in Algeria.

• Cocoa contains caffeine.

• The average American will eat 880 chickens, 14 cows, 23 pigs, 770 pounds of fish, 35 turkeys, and 12 sheep in his or her lifetime.

• Recipe for a Shirley Temple: a glass of ginger ale and a dash of grenadine, a non-alcoholic syrup made from pomegranates.

• If bottled mineral water were sold in oil barrels, it would sell for around $500 a barrel—about eight times the price of oil in 2006.

• Kool-Aid has been around since 1927, when its inventor changed the recipe for a soft-drink syrup called Fruit Smack into a powder to make it easier to ship.

ANIMAL RECORDS

• Highest skydive by a dog: 4,572 feet, by a dog named Brutus in 1997.

• Look who's gaining on you: The cheetah is the fastest land animal, with a top speed of 65 mph. (The fastest a human can run is 23 mph.)

• The blue whale has two claims to fame: It's the largest creature that's ever lived on Earth—bigger than any known dinosaur—and it's also the loudest. Its call, measured at 188 decibels, is louder than a commercial jet taking off.

• The Tanzanian parasitic wasp, the world's smallest winged insect, is smaller than a housefly's eye.

• Gray whales migrate farther than any other mammal—they travel about 12,000 miles every year.

• The world's smallest mammal? The bumblebee bat of Thailand. It weighs less than a penny.

• Sailfish are the fastest fish in the sea, clocked at 68 miles per hour.

• Weighing in at 100 pounds plus, the capybara, an Amazon mammal that looks like a huge guinea pig, is the world's largest rodent.

FLAGS

• The only national flag that's a solid color with no decoration: the green flag of Libya.

• The American colonies flew a flag during the American Revolution featuring a rattlesnake and the warning "Don't Tread on Me."

• The color most commonly found in national flags? Red.

• Napoleon designed the Italian flag; all he did was change the French red, white, and blue design to red, white, and green (his favorite color).

• "I give up!" A white flag is the universal symbol for surrender.

• Most pirate ships flew the Jolly Roger—a skull and crossbones on a black background—but Blackbeard the Pirate's flag showed a skeleton holding a spear pointed at a bleeding heart. Arrrrgh!

• A black flag in a car race is the signal for a driver to make a pit stop.

• In ancient Rome, a red flag was the signal for battle.

• When Russia stopped flying the Communist flag in 1991, it went back to its old flag—three horizontal stripes of white, blue, and red—designed in the 17th century during the reign of Czar Peter the Great.

STRANGE MUSEUMS

• The Cockroach Hall of Fame in Plano, Texas, features dead bugs dressed as celebrities and historical figures.

• The Burlingame Pez Museum in California will custom build a Pez dispenser in your image. All they need is a photo and $14.95.

• Don't miss the Inmate Art Collection at the Texas Prison Museum, in Huntsville. Uncle John's favorite? A bouquet of roses made out of toilet paper.

• The Beer Can Museum in East Taunton, Massachusetts, boasts a collection of 2,500 different beer cans, along with beer-can art and crafts, beer-can clothing, not to mention beer-can telephones and radios.

• The Lunchbox Museum in Columbus, Georgia, chronicles the TV-themed lunchboxes that kids carry to school. The collection includes over 3,500 boxes—from TV cowboy Hopalong Cassidy, who started it all, to the Brady Bunch Disco Fever lunchbox.

• Aw, nuts! The Nut Museum in Old Lyme, Connecticut, has closed its doors. But if you're nuts about nuts, you can still catch some of the museum's exhibits at the Connecticut College library in New London.

STUDIES SHOW...

• Weight lifters working out in gyms with blue walls can handle heavier weights.

• The first dinosaurs walked on their hind legs.

• Mosquitoes are more apt to bite people with smelly feet.

• Just like plants? Children grow faster in the spring.

• Nearly a third of Americans say they believe in reincarnation.

• Prairie dogs have a sophisticated language of short sounds, each equivalent to a sentence. Scientists have identified 10 nouns, including "hawk," "human," and "elk," and other words that describe the size, shape, and color of the intruder.

• Sorry to bug you, but your body probably contains traces of common pesticides like roach, termite, and flea killers.

• The average Japanese 11-year-old today is six inches taller than an average 11-year-old in 1950.

• Christmas countdown: On December 15, 2005, 85 toys were sold every minute on eBay.

• There is only one doctor for every 5,000 people in the world.

TRAVEL TIPS

• In Pakistan, it's impolite to show the soles of your feet or to point your foot when you're sitting on the floor.

• In Sri Lanka, *shaking* your head means "yes" and *nodding* your head means "no"—exactly the opposite of what Americans do.

• Japanese women cover their mouths when they laugh because showing one's teeth is considered rude.

• In Chile, slapping your right fist into your left palm is obscene, and an open palm with the fingers separated means "stupid."

• Never point at your head while you're behind the wheel in Italy. That gesture is offensive because it signals that you think another driver is stupid.

• In northern Germany, it's disrespectful to smile at a stranger on the street, since smiling is considered a demonstration of affection.

• In Japan, it's customary to study someone's business card carefully after they hand it to you; it's rude to look up too soon.

• In restaurants in Germany and Switzerland, don't be surprised if a stranger sits at an empty chair at your table. (And it's perfectly okay not to talk to your new tablemate.)

KNIGHTS IN SHINING ARMOR

• Knighthood is also known as "chivalry," which comes from the French word for knight, *chevalier*.

• The modern military salute comes from the days of chivalry (the 5th through 16th centuries), when armored knights would raise their visors to identify themselves when they rode past the king.

• Knights operated under a strict code of bravery, loyalty, and generosity.

• In medieval times, any man who trained to fight could become a knight. But the knight had to buy his own armor and weaponry—which were expensive—so most knights came from wealthy families.

• At seven years old, a boy could become a "page"—a knight's servant. From the knight he learned manners, religion, and how to handle horses and weapons.

• At 14, a page became a "squire," a personal aide and servant who went into battle with his knight. When a squire was fully trained, at 18 to 21 years old, he could become a knight.

• Any knight could bestow knighthood. The ceremony, a tap on the shoulder with a sword and the words "I dub thee knight," was called an "accolade," which today means praise or honor.

• Many medieval kings awarded land to knights who helped defend the kingdom. To keep their land, knights had to serve in the king's army for 40 days per year.

• Today in Great Britain, the queen bestows knighthood on men and women who've served England in outstanding ways. Men take on the title "Sir" and women are called "Dame." Here are some knights you might know:

Sir Sean Connery

Sir Paul McCartney

Dame Julie Andrews

Sir Ian McKellen

Sir Anthony Hopkins

Dame Elizabeth Taylor

Sir Elton John

SUGARY STUFF

• Sucralose, better known as Splenda, was discovered by a chemist who was trying to invent a new insecticide.

• All cats and most dogs cannot taste sugar.

• On average, Americans consume more that 140 pounds of cane sugar, corn syrup, and other natural sugars per year—50% more than the Germans and French, and nine times more than the Chinese.

• Saccharin, used in Sweet'N Low, is banned in Canada.

• Almost 300 billion pounds of sugar was consumed worldwide in 2005.

• A study to see if people would lose their taste for sugar if they gradually ate less and less of it had to be abandoned: The subjects couldn't stay off sugar. (The experiment did work for salt, though.)

• Newborn babies love sugar; in fact, a little sugar in water relaxes them.

• Scientists are trying to develop a way to increase the sweetness of sugar—without increasing the calories—so that less of it can be used in recipes.

• Aspartame, used in the sugar substitute Equal, causes cancer in rats—but not in people.

ODORAMA

Fascinating facts about farts.

• Another name for farting: *flatulence.*

• Burp, burp, fart, burp, fart, fart, burp, fart, burp, fart—10 down, 5 to go. Most of us (including you) burp or fart as least 10 to 15 times per day.

• Beans are famous for making you fart, but cauliflower, broccoli, apples, milk, raisins, and popcorn can make you fart even more than beans do.

• A fart smells the same to the farter and the farted-at. But since the fart blasts away from the farter, the other guy usually smells it first.

• A fart can take 30 to 45 minutes to travel through your body. *Bon voyage*, and be sure to let us know (loudly) when it gets to the end of its trip.

• If farts could be measured like water, the gas you pass each day would amount to between one cup and one half gallon.

• Picture this: You're up in space without a spacesuit. And you fart. Hang on, because the force is enough to propel you forward through space.

• If you soak dried beans in water for twelve hours before cooking, they'll produce less flatulence.

• It may not be ladylike, but the fact is that women fart three times more often than men.

WEIRD WEATHER

• Hailstones the size of bowling balls fell on Coffeyville, Kansas, on September 2, 1970.

• Great balls of fire: Thousands of people have reported seeing what's called "ball lightning"—glowing balls that are as bright as light bulbs—flying though the sky, or even entering their houses.

• In 1979 a thunderstorm in Norwich, England, generated 2- to 4-inch flakes of ice that fluttered out of the sky like falling leaves.

• Whirlwinds (or "dust devils") usually just carry sand and debris, but they've also been known to suck up flames from nearby forest fires and carry them away.

• Golf-ball-size hailstones fell in Alberta, Canada, in 1953, killing 36,000 ducks—not to be confused with a 1933 storm in Worcester, Massachusetts, that generated huge hailstones that contained *freshly frozen* ducks.

• The secondary rainbow in a double rainbow is the exact reverse of the primary rainbow: The red is on the inner edge and the blue is on the outer edge.

• An 1877 issue of *Scientific American* reported a rain of snakes, some as big as 1½ feet long, that fell out of the sky in Memphis, Tennessee.

• A "sun dog" is a bright spot in the sky that's 22 degrees to the left or right of the sun.

PLACES OF INTEREST

• Where are they? “Land of the Midnight Sun,” “Land of Enchantment,” and “Land of 10,000 Lakes,” are the nicknames of Alaska, New Mexico, and Minnesota, respectively.

• What city has the most telescopes in the world? Tucson, Arizona.

• The first log cabins in North America were built in 1683 by Swedish immigrants in Delaware.

• Coolest state? It could be Florida. In 1851 Dr. John Gorrie of Apalachicola, Florida, patented the process of manufacturing ice.

• In a competition for “Longest Main Street in the United States,” Island Park, Idaho, would win: Its main street is 33 miles long.

• In 1928, Baltimore, Maryland, became the home of the first umbrella factory in America.

• Visit the Elephant Hall in the University of Nebraska State Museum in Lincoln, Nebraska, and you’ll see the world’s largest collection of elephant skeletons.

• The next time someone you know gets a parking ticket, tell them to blame it on Oklahoma City, Oklahoma. That’s where, in 1935, the first parking meter was installed.

CREEPY QUIZ

Q: Why do mosquitoes bite?

A: They need the protein in blood to produce their eggs—that's why only female mosquitoes bite.

Q: Beehives seem like pretty busy places, but how many bees have been known fit into one hive?

A: A beehive can contain as many as 80,000 bees at a time.

Q: Is it true that doctors once used bloodsucking leeches as a medical treatment for sick people?

A: Yes. Back in the 1800s, doctors thought leeches could drain "bad blood" from sick patients. The practice was so widespread that leeches became an endangered species. (Some doctors still use them.)

Q: How many legs does the biggest centipede have?

A: The biggest, *Scolopendra gigantea*, only has 46 legs, but other centipedes have as many as 350. Millipedes can have up to 750 legs!

Q: Why doesn't a mayfly have a mouth?

A: Because it has a life span of only one or two days, and doesn't eat. (It does eat in its immature stage, when it's called a *naiad*.)

LOONY LAWS

- It's against the law to sing off-key in North Carolina.
- You may be headed straight for jail if you dare to wear New York Jets clothing in Ada, Oklahoma.
- Don't box with a kangaroo in Myrtle Creek, Oregon. The law forbids it. (There are kangaroos in Oregon?)
- It's illegal to sleep on top of a refrigerator outdoors in Pennsylvania.
- Curb your appetite! No one is allowed to bite off another person's leg in Rhode Island.
- In Charleston, South Carolina, the fire department is legally permitted to blow up your house.
- In Texas, it's illegal to sell your eye.
- It may be inconvenient, but you're not allowed to wash your mule on the sidewalk in Culpeper, Virginia.
- Kirkland, Illinois, law forbids bees to fly through any of its streets. (Has anyone told the bees?)
- Whew! It's against the law for a monster to enter the city limits of Urbana, Illinois.
- In Zion, Illinois, you are not permitted to give lighted cigars to dogs, cats, or other animals kept as pets.
- It's illegal to go whale fishing in Nebraska.

• In Hartford, Connecticut, it's against the law to educate a dog.

• In Chicago, Illinois, you're breaking the law if you fish in your pajamas.

• You'll just have to let your nose run in Waterville, Maine, because it's illegal to blow it in public.

• In Louisiana, it's against the law to gargle in public.

• The state of Massachusetts absolutely forbids dueling with water pistols.

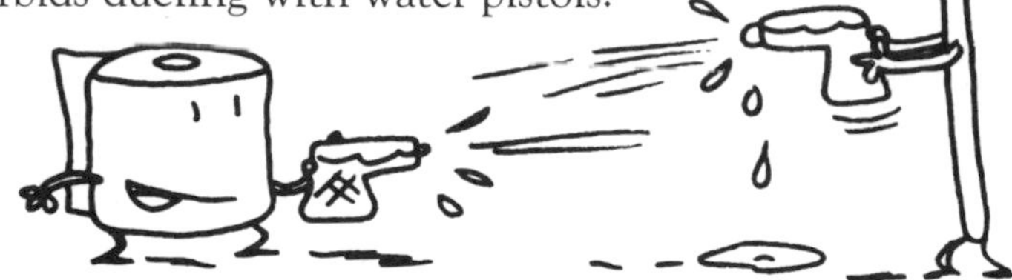

• Not that you'd want to, but teasing skunks is against the law in Minnesota.

• If a child burps during a church service in Omaha, Nebraska, his or her parents may be arrested.

• In New Jersey, it's illegal to slurp your soup.

• Oklahoma law prohibits anyone from making "ugly faces" at dogs.

• Don't whistle underwater in Vermont. It's against the law. (But how do you do it, anyway?)

• According to Washington State law, you may not pretend your parents are rich.

• In Mesquite, Texas, it's illegal for children to have "unusual haircuts."

HANDY NUMBERS

• In a group of 23 people, there is a 50% chance that two of them will have the same birthday.

• When it's written out as "forty," 40 is the only number whose letters are in alphabetical order.

• A two-inch-diameter garden hose will carry four times as much water as a one-inch-diameter hose.

• If a person had started counting the moment they were born and continued without stopping until they turned 65, they still wouldn't have counted to a billion.

• Roll the dice. If one die reads "three," what's on the opposite side? Four. How do you know? The numbers on opposite sides of a die always add up to seven.

• In case you ever want to call the White House with a comment, the phone number is (202) 456-1111.

• Try this on a calculator: What is 11,111,111 multiplied by itself? 123,456,787,654,321

• If you counted all the black spots on all the dalmations in every scene of *101 Dalmatians*, you'd see 6,469,952 of them.

• To date, the year 1888 requires the most Roman numerals: MDCCCLXXXVIII.

HAIL TO THE CHIEF

• In a survey of 500 historians, Warren G. Harding was voted the worst president in American history.

• President Andrew Jackson believed the Earth was flat.

• The tallest president was 6'4" Abe Lincoln; the shortest was James Madison, at 5'4".

• Julie Nixon, daughter of 37th president Richard Nixon, is married to David Eisenhower, grandson of 34th president Dwight Eisenhower.

• President Jimmy Carter's boyhood home was built from plans purchased from a Sears catalog.

• The U.S. interstate highway system was the brainchild of President Dwight D. Eisenhower, who based the idea on the German *autobahns* (highways) he'd seen after World War II.

• The president gets a 21-gun salute; the vice president gets only 19.

• **Q:** Which U.S. president served for only 32 days?
A: William Henry Harrison. On his inauguration day, he caught a cold that developed into fatal pneumonia.

• James Buchanan was the only bachelor president. Ronald Reagan was the only president who had been divorced.

AMAZING ENGINEERING

• How much soil had to be dug out to create the Panama Canal? More than 175 million cubic yards.

• The Chinese used rice flour to strengthen the bricks when they were building the Great Wall.

• The Eiffel Tower—the tallest structure in the world when it was completed in 1889—was built just to show that iron could be as strong as stone…but much lighter.

• The first paved road was built around 2500 B.C. in Egypt. The ancient Egyptians used it to haul stones for the construction of the pyramids.

• The deepest hole ever dug is in Russia, on the Kola Peninsula. Its purpose: to research the structure of the earth's crust. Its depth: 7 miles.

• It took more than 10 million bricks to build the Empire State Building.

• Who's taller? It happened in 1929 in New York City: Just when the Manhattan Trust Company finished what they thought was the world's tallest building, workers at the Chrysler Building hoisted a spire—hidden inside the building—up through the top of the roof to steal the coveted title.

ROCKOLOGY

According to folklore, some gemstones have special powers.

• **Agate** worn in jewelry was supposed to make other people believe you and to ward off bad dreams.

• **Lapis lazuli** could help to break down barriers, allowing people to go beyond their limitations.

• **Clear quartz crystal** was said to contain images of the future. (But few "crystal" balls at carnivals are really crystal—they're usually made of glass.)

• **Amber** (petrified tree sap) held in the hand was believed to help people think more clearly.

• **Bloodstone** got its name because of the belief that it would stop the flow of blood from a wound.

• **Moonstones** were thought to help you understand your feelings better and act on them decisively.

• **Citrine** was supposed to make people more creative.

• **Malachite** was believed to focus the mind and make life's changes easier.

• **Jade** is still associated with positive energy. At one time it was thought to be a healing stone that promoted charity, modesty, wisdom, serenity, and love.

• **Rose quartz** was said to encourage caring and reduce anger. It was considered a wonderful gift to present to anyone you loved.

HEALTHY LIVING

• If you walk an extra 20 minutes every day, over a year you'll burn off seven pounds of body fat. (Unless you're walking to McDonald's.)

• Scientists have determined that having guilty feelings may actually damage your immune system.

• Listening to music is good for digestion.

• Average life span during the Middle Ages: less than 30 years. We're getting healthier: Today it's about 65.

• Vegetarians make up about 25% of the world's population.

• Four out of five 10-year-old American girls have already been on a diet.

• To stay healthy, the average person needs 37 grams of protein a day.

• 12% of Switzerland's population is obese, compared to over 30% in the U.S.

• More than 40% of American women use hand moisturizer three times a day or more.

• 13% of Brits are on a diet at any given time; at least twice that many Americans are.

• One out of every 15 kids under 18 has asthma.

• Walking on hard dirt burns more calories—7% more—than walking on pavement.

NUMBER ONES

• Officially, "bacteria" is plural; one bacteria is a "bacterium."

• In 2005 Germany surpassed the United States to become the world's number-one exporter.

• The word "one" has appeared in the titles of more than 500 movies.

• Odd fact? The ancient Greeks considered the number 1 to be both odd and even. They regarded the number 3 as the first odd number.

• The word "hiccup" appears exactly once in the works of Shakespeare.

• Only one U.S. president has had the astrological sign Gemini: George H.W. Bush.

• The first Nobel Peace Prize was awarded in 1901 to Jean Henri Dunant, founder of the Red Cross.

• One human being out of five (on the entire planet) is a Chinese farmer.

• Creepy fact: You can fit 1,815 standard-size graves into one acre of land.

• Nottingham, England, was the first city to have braille signs in its shopping malls.

• The average Haitian spends one minute per year making international phone calls.

REPTILES

• Iguanas can stay underwater for nearly 30 minutes.

• Crocodiles dig underground burrows in extremely hot weather…and can live in them for several months without eating or drinking.

• All reptiles are vertebrates, meaning they have a backbone. And except for snakes and a few lizards, they all have four legs.

• Snakes don't have ears like other animals, but they have inner ears that sense ground vibrations.

• Reptiles don't perspire, and they don't have any sweat glands in their skin.

• The brain of a reptile accounts for less than 1% of its body mass.

• How do they pull their heads and legs inside their shells? Turtles are the only animals whose hips and shoulders are inside their rib cages.

• Some lizards have a "third eye," a tiny, light-sensitive, transparent structure on top of the head that helps them regulate how long they stay in the sun.

• Snakes have no eyelids; transparent eye "caps" protect their eyes.

• We've all got one: The lowest part of your brain stem is called the "reptilian brain." It's the part of your brain that controls survival instincts.

IF YOU SAY SO

How hard can it be to learn Japanese? All the kids in Japan do it. Here are a few words to get you started.

• *Pika* means "flash of light" in Japanese, and *chu* is the squeak of a mouse. So the Pókemon name Pikachu literally means "flashing mouse squeak."

• First-grade students in Japan are called *pika-pika ichi nen sei*, or "shiny first graders."

• Rice is so popular in Japan that the words for breakfast, lunch, and dinner literally translate as "morning rice," "noon rice," and "evening rice."

• Some Japanese animal sounds: Pig: *buu-buu*. Dog: *wan-wan*. Frog: *kero-kero*. Rooster: *ko ke kokkou*.

• In Japanese, *kara* means "empty." So *karate* means "empty hand" (no weapon) and *karaoke* means "empty orchestra" (no voice).

• The Japanese love to shorten phrases, especially foreign ones. "Remote control" is *rimokon* (pronounced ree-mo-cone). "Schwarzenegger" is *Shuwa-chan*. And "Brad Pitt" is *Burapi* (that seems longer, but the Japanese pronunciation of his full name has five syllables).

• The Japanese word for "meow" is *nyan-nyan*. So the catlike Pókemon, Meowth, is called Nyasu in Japan.

• We say "two peas in a pod" to describe two nearly identical things. In Japanese, it's "two cucumbers."

BASEBALL TEAM NAMES

• "Mets" is short for "Metropolitans," taken from the team's corporate name, The New York Metropolitan Baseball Club, Inc.

• Not so "innocent," after all: The Pittsburgh Pirates were called the Innocents until 1891, when the team "stole" second baseman Lou Bierbauer from the Philadelphia Athletics. Bierbauer's former fans started calling the team the Pirates, and it stuck.

• In the 1890s, Cleveland's team was called the Spiders. One of their players, Louis Sockalexis, was a Native American, so fans started calling the team the "Indians." The name was officially changed in 1913.

• At first the Astros were called the Colt .45s, but when Houston got its new NASA Space Center in 1965, Astros seemed more appropriate.

• The Minnesota Twins are named after the "twin cities" of Minneapolis and St. Paul.

• If you know anything about Milwaukee, you'll know it's home to lots of beer breweries; the Milwaukee Brewers seemed like a natural choice.

TONGUE TWISTERS

The kind you have to say free times thast…tree thimes… Oh, you know what we mean.

- Sixish.
- The sixth sick sheik's sixth sheep's sick.
- Truly rural.
- Betty better butter Brad's bread.
- Greek grapes.
- Mrs. Smith's Fish Sauce Shop.
- Peggy Babcock.
- Toy boat. Toy boat. Toy boat.
- Flash message!
- Moose noshing much mush.
- Knapsack straps.
- Girl gargoyle, guy gargoyle.
- Three free throws.
- The epitome of femininity.
- Thieves seize skis.
- The myth of Miss Muffet.
- Fat frogs flying past.
- Freshly fried flying fish.

CRIME AND PUNISHMENT

• How many police officers are there in the United States? About 561,000.

• The most: New York City has more than 30,000 officers.

• The rest: 90% of the nation's police departments have fewer than 25 officers.

• The FBI has more than 200,000,000 fingerprints on file.

• 70% of all violent crimes are committed by only 6% of the criminal population.

• The results of a lie-detector test are not allowed as evidence in most U.S. courts.

• Shoplifters in the United States pocket $35 million worth of merchandise every day.

• In a police lineup, the suspects are numbered 2 through 9; no one wears the number 1. Why? So no one person looks any guiltier than the others.

• Thefts from vending machines cost the soft-drink industry $100 million a year.

• Out of every six robberies, one involves a robber who knows the victim.

• Most burglaries occur during the daytime.

• In Finland, a man once got a $200,000 speeding ticket. Why? Because in Finland, traffic fines are based on the income of the offender...and the speeder's family was extremely rich. (They owned a sausage company.)

• In 1985, a woman was accused of stealing a basketball. It turned out that she was pregnant.

• The most common excuse drivers give police officers after they're caught speeding: "I didn't see the sign."

• Have you heard the term "M.O." on a cop show? It stands for *modus operandi*, which is Latin for "method of operating."

• Forensic fact: Police have a special type of wax that can lift a shoe print from snow.

• 53% of people polled believe the police are good at catching criminals.

• Middle children are less likely to end up in prison than first- and last-born children.

• Pink in the clink: There's a color called "Jailhouse Pink" that's been proven to soothe angry prisoners—but it only works for about half an hour.

• In 2004 a woman was arrested for trying to pass a $1 million bill at a Wal-Mart in Georgia. (It was fake—there's no such thing as a $1 million bill.)

• A police sergeant in Texas was fired for taking a soda from the refrigerator in a house he was searching.

BIG CATS

• When cheetahs run, they appear to be flying because most of the time all four feet are off the ground.

• Tigers like to attack from behind. To prevent attacks, farmers in India wear masks with eyes on the back of their heads.

• Snow leopards who live in the Himalayan mountains have such long tails that they can wrap themselves in them for warmth.

• A lion's muzzle is like a fingerprint—no two have the same pattern of whiskers.

• Lions usually roar in the hours between dusk and dawn.

• Big cats live almost twice as long in captivity as in the wild.

• A lion's scientific name is *Panthera leo*, a tiger's is *Panthera tigris*.

• A black panther isn't a separate species: It's simply a jaguar, leopard, or puma that's black.

• Mountain lions don't roar—they whistle or shriek.

• Tigers are the largest members of the cat family, and the Siberian tiger is the largest of them all.

• Cheetahs don't growl, but they make other kinds of noises, like yelping and humming and even purring.

DOWN UNDER

From the land that gave us kangaroos, koalas, and Crocodile Dundee.

• Why are the emu and kangaroo both on the Australian coat of arms? Because neither can walk backwards, thus signifying the forward-thinking character of Australians.

• The only mammals that don't give birth to live young are native to Australia. The platypus and the echidna (a.k.a. the spiny anteater) lay eggs.

• Australia is the only continent on Earth without an active volcano.

• The first settlers from England, who arrived in 1788, included 717 convicts and their military guards; 180 of the convicts were women.

• Aboriginal peoples and natives of the Torres Strait Islands off the northern coast of Australia account for about 2% of the country's population.

• The school year in Australia starts in late January and ends mid-December for the Christmas (summer!) break.

• One out of four Australians was born in another country.

• Cute, but wrong: Baby platypuses aren't called "puggles" as many people believe. They have no official name, but "platypup" has been suggested.

IMAS

Instant Messaging Abbreviations, Silly.

• WUF	Where are you from?
• A3	Anytime, Anyplace, Anywhere
• B4N	Bye for now
• C&G	Chuckle and grin
• DIKU	Do I know you?
• DLTBBB	Don't let the bedbugs bite
• EG	Evil grin
• GR8	Great!
• K	OK
• L8R G8R	Later, gator
• ::POOF::	Goodbye
• UOK	Are you OK?
• ROFLOL	Rolling on the floor laughing out loud
• QPSA?	*¿Que pasa?* (How's it going?)
• S^	'S up? (What's up?)
• SUAKM	Shut up and kiss me
• U4E	Yours forever
• WDALYIC	Who died and left you in charge?
• WE	Whatever
• WIBAMU	Well, I'll be a monkey's uncle

THE HIMALAYAS

No, it's not a rock group. It's a mountain range in Asia—and the ultimate climbing challenge for us earthlings.

• Nine of the 10 highest mountains in the world—including Mt. Everest—are in the Himalayas.

• The rocks that make up the Himalayan mountains were an ancient sea floor until about 40 million years ago when, in a process called "uplifting," the sea floor was forced upward.

• The Himalayas are still growing—at a rate of about 2.4 inches a year.

• Because the planet isn't a perfect sphere, the point farthest from the center of the Earth is the summit of Mt. Chimborazo in Ecuador, not the top of Mt. Everest.

• The snowfields of the Himalayas are permanent—they never melt, not even in the summer.

• Everest's name in Nepal is *Sagarmatha* (goddess of the sky), and in Tibet it's called *Chomolungma* (mother goddess of the universe).

• Once known as Peak 15, Mt. Everest was named after Sir George Everest, a British surveyor-general of India. He pronounced his name EEV-rest.

• First skier to descend from the peak: Davo Karnicar of Slovenia in 2000. It took him five hours of uninterrupted skiing.

STRANGE SUPERSTITIONS

- In Tibet, the number 42 is considered sacred.
- What's the Mexican version of the Tooth Fairy? The Tooth Mouse!
- The ancient Egyptians believed that black cats had divine powers.
- 84% of Americans say they believe in miracles.
- *Phrenology* is the belief that the size and shape of a person's head determines their character. According to phrenologists, the bumps on your head reveal 42 aspects of your personality.
- Storks are considered symbols of good luck. And according to folklore, it's the stork that delivers every new baby.
- According to legend, emeralds have the power to ward off evil spirits.
- Some people believe that dreaming about a dove will bring you happiness.
- According to ancient Egyptian mythology, the fate of the dead is decided by a group of 42 demons.
- In Asia, cranes are revered as symbols of long life.
- Superstitious people think an itchy nose means you'll have a quarrel with someone.

A VISIT TO MICROBIA

Let's pull up a microscope and visit the land of bacteria, fungi, viruses, and their friends.

• A teaspoon of dirt from your backyard contains more than 1,000,000,000 bacteria. So does a quart of dirty bathwater.

• A virus is a tiny bit of DNA or RNA wrapped in a protein coat.

• There's a fungus among us: Bread mold, athlete's foot, yeast, and penicillin are all types of fungus.

• Free-floating viruses are "inert" (inactive) until they come into contact with a living cell—that's when they come to life and can begin attacking.

• Antibiotics, the drugs commonly used to kill bacteria, do not affect viruses at all.

• Scientists have revived bacteria that had been dormant for 250 million years.

• A type of giant amoeba—named *Chaos chaos*—can be seen with the naked eye.

• A mushroom is a fungus's reproductive organ.

• Oh, is that all? About 200 million years passed between the appearance of bacteria on Earth and the next evolutionary step: single-celled organisms with a nucleus.

SURVEY SAYS...

- 56% of men would like to wear a suit of armor.
- 27% of people wish their first kiss had been with someone else.
- 49% of people believe that polls tell the truth.
- 50% of American women prefer to sit with their legs crossed.
- 59% of schoolchildren claim that their parents nag constantly.
- 82% of teens worry about tests.
- 81% of teenage girls say the idea of growing old alone doesn't bother them.
- Only 15% of adults think journalists tell the truth.
- No! 66% of 16-year-olds say they are pessimists.
- 27% of female lottery winners admit to hiding the winning ticket in their bra.
- 31% of workers don't eat any lunch.
- Of all the candles sold, women purchase 96% of them.
- How many snorers in your household? 71% report they have at least one.
- People in low-income homes spend 50% more time playing video games than people in high-income homes.

ENDANGERED SPECIES

- Between 1919 and 1921, nearly 108 million animals were killed for the American fur trade.
- During the first 20 years of the Endangered Species Act, 632 species were listed endangered. Today the number is around 500.
- The first animal conservation laws were instituted by Chinese emperor Kublai Khan in the 13th century.
- There are only 3,000 manatees, also known as "sea cows," remaining in Florida. (They're related to elephants, not cows.)
- Only about 1,600 pandas survive in the wild today—and only in China.
- Melting sea ice due to climate change leaves less time and area for endangered polar bears to hunt for food and store it.
- There are fewer than 800 nenes—Hawaii's state bird—left in the Hawaiian Islands.
- Here's some good news: In 1800 more than 50 million bison roamed the plains of North America. By 1890 only 800 were left, but now the numbers have been built back up to about 130,000.
- Scientists believe that one species becomes extinct every 20 minutes.

THE CLOTHES CLOSET

• An 8,000-year-old sandal found in a cave in Missouri is the oldest known footwear in the world.

• Mexican sombreros are meant to provide shade for the entire body.

• American men buy 35 articles of clothing a year. American women buy 54.

• Wal-Mart sells more clothing than all other department stores combined.

• How many gallons does a 10-gallon hat hold? Not even one.

• Farmington, Maine, holds a parade on the first Saturday in December to honor Chester Greenwood, the boy who invented earmuffs.

• The woolen swimsuits that people wore at the turn of the 20th century weighed about 20 pounds when wet.

• Men carried purses before women did. The purses were called "pockets." But because they hung from a string and could be easily stolen, eventually they were sewn inside clothing and—*voilà!*—became the pockets we can't live without today.

• The first knit socks were discovered in Egyptian tombs of the 3rd–6th centuries A.D.

ANIMAL QUIZ

Q: If you see a moose kneeling, what's he doing?

A: Eating. He can't graze like a cow—his neck is too short and his legs are too long—so he has to kneel to eat.

Q: If it has one horn, it's from Africa; if it has two horns, it's from India. What is it?

A: A rhino.

Q: Dogs are color-blind when it comes to seeing green and red, so how do seeing-eye dogs tell the difference between a red traffic light and a green one?

A: They don't. Instead, they watch the flow of traffic to see when it's safe to cross.

Q: Are zebras white with black stripes or vice versa?

A: Scientists are still arguing about it.

Q: What kind of fish is a Portuguese Man-of-War?

A: It's not actually a fish—it's an invertebrate, meaning it doesn't have a backbone like a true fish does. It's related to both jellyfish and coral. The Man-of-War isn't really even one single animal: It's a colony of four parts that work together to survive.

YOU NAME IT

• Greenland isn't very green—in fact, it's almost entirely covered with snow and ice. Viking explorers named it Greenland to lure settlers there.

• It's the yellow soil beneath China's Yellow River that gave it its name.

• The Dead Sea really is dead. Located at the end of the Jordan River, the sea's water evaporates and leaves heavy deposits of minerals, which makes it uninhabitable and much saltier than an ocean.

• The Ivory Coast in northwest Africa was once the center of the ivory trade for Europeans, who hunted elephants for their valuable ivory tusks.

• Why is the Red Sea called "red"? It could be from the occasional red algae that appear there, or it could have been named for nearby red mountains. Some people say it's actually a mistranslation of "Reed Sea."

• Huh? The Canary Islands were named for the wild dogs that lived there. You've heard dogs called "canines"? *Canis* is Latin for "dog"—and the ancient Romans named the islands.

• Ireland is called the Emerald Isle because of its green countryside, not because of any actual emeralds.

• Moscow's Red Square isn't red: It was so named because *red* means "beautiful" in Russian.

AMUSEMENT PARKS

• There are more than 1,300 roller coasters in North America.

• Faster than a speeding bullet? The "Superman: The Escape" roller coaster at Six Flags Magic Mountain in California accelerates to 100 mph in 7 seconds.

• The Ferris wheel was the brainchild—and namesake—of George Ferris, a bridge builder from Pittsburgh, Pennsylvania. The wheel debuted at the Chicago World's Fair in 1893.

• The world's tallest roller coaster, Kingda Ka at Great Adventure in New Jersey, reaches its peak at 456 feet. It's the world's fastest, too—clocked at 128 mph.

• A 14-year-old German boy built a 300-foot-long *working* roller coaster in his backyard over the summer of 2005...but local officials made him tear it down.

• That whoopsy feeling you get when you float out of your seat on a roller coaster is called "airtime."

• The world's oldest operating amusement park—Bakken Amusement Park in Denmark—first opened for business in 1583.

• Insider's name for high-speed spinning rides like the Tilt-A-Whirl: "Spin-N-Barf"

SPORTS BY THE NUMBERS

• How high the hoop: In pro basketball, the hoop is exactly 10 feet high.

• When the word "ski" is mentioned, three out of five Americans say that Colorado is the first place they think of.

• In major league baseball, the pitcher's plate is 10 inches above the level of home plate. The pitcher's mound is 18 feet across.

• The fastest recorded tennis serve? 153 miles per hour.

• The hurdles in the women's 100-meter hurdle event are 33 inches high. In the men's 400-meter hurdles, they're 36 inches high. Which is only fair because on average, men are 3 inches taller than women.

• Old-time baseball player Hughie Jennings holds the records for being hit by the most pitches (287 times) and for being hit the most in a single season (51).

• Take that! A professional boxing glove weighs eight ounces.

• The top rope surrounding a boxing ring is 52 inches high.

• The length of a bowling lane is 60 feet from the foul line to the center of the first pin.

DEAR DAIRY

• In Spain, people pour chocolate milk or coffee on breakfast cereal.

• The average American drinks 400 glasses of milk per year.

• Roughly one in seven people is lactose intolerant, which means they have trouble digesting milk.

• Every year, the Kraft company makes enough Cool Whip to fill the Grand Canyon.

• Love cheese? You'll probably eat more than a ton—2,000 pounds—of it in your lifetime.

• It takes 29 cups of milk to make one pound of butter.

• Butter's yellow color comes from the beta-carotene in the grass that dairy cows eat. Butter is yellower in the summer, when grass is plentiful. In winter, it's usually off-white.

• People added carrot juice to butter in the Middle Ages, thinking it made the color more attractive.

• Need something to cool off your mouth after eating spicy food? Try milk—it contains *casein*, a protein that soothes burning taste buds.

• Bad, but still good: Blue cheese was most likely discovered by accident centuries ago, when cheese was stored in caves. A batch of cheese probably got moldy, and some brave person decided to taste it anyway.

BIG CITIES

• Istanbul, Turkey, is the only city in the world located on two continents: Europe and Asia.

• Los Angeles's full name—El Pueblo de Nuestra Señora la Reina de los Angeles de Porciuncula—can be abbreviated to 3.63% of its size: L.A.

• The first city to reach a population of 1 million was Rome, Italy, in 133 B.C.

• In the year 1900, the largest cities by population were London, England (6.5 million), New York City (4.2 million), and Paris, France (3.3 million).

• The largest city in Africa: Cairo, with a population of over 7 million.

• 36% of New York City's 8 million people are foreign-born; 41% of Los Angeles's 4 million people are.

• Shanghai, China, has the highest population of any city in the world: over 14 million.

• New York City was nicknamed "the Big Apple" by jazz musicians of the 1930s, who used the slang expression "apple" for any town or city. Therefore, to play New York was to play the big time.

ANIMALS IN CAPTIVITY

• Sea World owns 25 orcas—55% of the worldwide total in captivity. And, by the way, they're not killer "whales," they're a type of dolphin.

• A zoo gorilla named Jambo made headlines in 1986 when a five-year-old boy fell into the gorilla enclosure and lost consciousness. Jambo placed himself protectively between the little guy and the other gorillas until he was rescued.

• Watch your hands: In 2004 a piranha was discovered living in a petting-zoo aquarium in Berlin, Germany.

• Jungle gym: Zookeepers in Anchorage, Alaska, installed a treadmill to help an elephant named Maggie lose some weight. The treadmill and a diet helped Maggie lose 1,000 pounds, down from 9,000.

• Zoo authorities in England sent a parrot into solitary confinement after the bird used some really bad language directed at two policemen, a mayor, and a priest. (They can't figure out how he learned it.)

• About a month before St. Patrick's Day in 2004, two polar bears in the Singapore Zoo turned green. A zoo spokesperson explained that it was because of harmless algae growing in their hollow hair shafts, and could be easily cured with a salt solution.

SOUND EFFECTS

• The people who create sound effects for movies are called "Foley artists." Sometimes they use very bizarre objects to find just the right sound, like snapping celery sticks to mimic the sound of bones being broken.

• In *Star Wars*, Chewbacca's voice is a combination of sounds from a bear, badger, walrus, and camel.

• The sound of the tornado in *Twister* is a recording of camel moaning played back at slow speed.

• The background crowd noise in a movie or television show is called a *walla*. The term comes from the early days of radio (before TV), when dramas were performed. A group of actors would repeat the word "walla" over and over again, which was supposed to sound like the murmur of a crowd. Today's walla actors use real words and conversations.

• In *The Matrix*, for the slow-motion shots where bullets slow down and the camera whips around, the sound designer put real bullets on strings and whirled them around to create the "whoosh" sound in the background.

• The ape's roar in *King Kong* is a lion's roar played at half speed, backwards.

• In *E.T. The Extra-Terrestrial*, the sound of E.T.'s waddling walk was created by squeezing a wet T-shirt stuffed with Jell-O.

WE'VE GOT CHEMISTRY

• Elements named for famous scientists: einsteinium (after Albert Einstein) and fermium (after Enrico Fermi).

• Chlorine will keep your swimming pool clean, but its first use was as a chemical weapon in World War I.

• Superman's home planet was named after the real element krypton, a gas that was discovered in 1898.

• Though it's commonly thought to have an icky smell—kind of like rotten eggs—sulfur is nearly odorless. The stuff that smells bad is *hydrogen sulfide*, a gas that forms in sewers and swamps.

• Neon is colorless, but gives off a red-orange glow when it's put in a vacuum tube and electricity is passed through it for a neon sign.

• Plastic is an organic compound, but it's usually considered an inorganic material because it takes so long—centuries—to decompose.

• Mercury is one of only five elements that are liquid at room temperature. The others are *caesium*, *francium*, *gallium*, and *bromine*.

• The full chemical name of *tryptophan synthetase* (an amino acid) is 1,909 letters long.

• Metals that are resistant to corrosion—such as gold, silver, and platinum—are called "noble" metals.

WHATCHA-MACALLIT, USA

Some real places in America.

• **Deathball Rock, Oregon**, was named after an especially bad batch of biscuits.

• **Atlasta Creek, Alaska.** A local woman was so delighted that a building had been constructed in this remote area that she exclaimed, "At last, a house!" The name stuck.

• **Norwood, Massachusetts.** A local man christened the town "Norwood" because it "had a pleasing sound, was easy to write, and had no *i* to dot or *t* to cross."

• **Matrimony Creek, North Carolina**, got its name from an unhappy surveyor who said the creek was irritatingly noisy—the same opinion he had of marriage.

• **Tesla, California's,** founding fathers named the town for inventor Nikola Tesla in hopes that their proposed power plant would supply electricity to San Francisco and make them rich. The plant was never built, and Tesla is now a ghost town.

• **Hot Coffee, Mississippi,** as you might imagine, was named in honor of a roadside store that sold *really* good coffee.

• **Rego Park, New York,** was named for a local construction company called Rego—short for "real good."

ALL OVER THE MAP

• Ho-Ho-Kus, New Jersey, is the only town in the United States that has two dashes in its name.

• Bolivia was named after Colombian-born freedom fighter Simón Bolívar (full name: Simón José Antonio de la Santísima Trinidad Bolívar Palacios y Blanco).

• Siberia means "sleeping land."

• Thailand translates to "land of the free."

• In 190 A.D., Roman emperor Commodus changed the name of Rome to Colonia Commodiana (Commodus's Colony). After he was assassinated a year later, the Senate changed the name back to Rome.

• The Bronx, New York, was named for its first European settler, Jonas Bronck.

• Bangkok's official Thai name is 167 letters long.

• Venezuela was named after Venice, Italy. The name literally means "Little Venice."

• St. Paul, Minnesota, was originally called "Pig's Eye," which was the nickname of Pierre Parrant, the city's first settler (and a notorious whiskey merchant).

• Istanbul, Turkey, was once called Constantinople after Roman emperor Constantine. But it was founded by Greeks who named it Byzantium…after King Byzas.

THE AVERAGE...

- ...roll of toilet paper is 114.8 feet long.
- ...human body has 29 feet of intestines.
- ...person laughs 17 times a day.
- ...American consumer spends $1,508 on clothes every year.
- ...ratio of yellow kernels to white kernels in a bag of popcorn is 9 to 1.
- ...Frenchman drinks 140 bottles of wine per year.
- ...American uses about 100 gallons of water a day.
- ...cat has 24 whiskers (12 on each side).
- ...adult human body contains 28 pounds of carbon.
- ...adult has approximately 45 *billion* fat cells in his or her body.
- ...whole chicken from the grocery store weighs 3 pounds, 12 ounces.
- ...person has about 25 moles on their body.
- ...iceberg weighs 20 tons.
- ...water droplet contains 100 quintillion water molecules. (That's 100,000,000,000,000,000,000.)
- ...American police officer will walk 1,632 miles on the job this year.

OH, HONEY!

Sweet facts about bees and honey.

- A honeybee will make only 1/12 of a teaspoon of honey in its entire lifetime (about four months).
- Worker honeybees have the toughest job in the hive—gathering the nectar for the honey. To make just one pound of honey, they will fly more than 55,000 miles and visit two million flowers.
- Honeybees "dance" to communicate with each other. When a worker bee returns to the hive with nectar, it gives everyone a taste and then, through its dance, it tells the other bees the location, quantity, and quality of the nectar supply.
- Even though their wings beat very fast, honeybees fly only about 15 miles per hour.
- European colonists introduced the honeybee to North America in 1638. Native Americans called it "white man's fly."
- Aside from adding it as an ingredient in food or drinks, American colonists used honey to make cement, varnish, medicine, and furniture polish.
- Not only did ancient Egyptians use honey to sweeten their bread, but they also fed it to sacred animals.
- In the Middle Ages, German peasants sometimes paid their rent with honey and beeswax.

NOT-SO-FAMOUS PEOPLE

- Astronomer Carolyn Shoemaker has discovered 32 comets and approximately 300 asteroids.
- Every photograph of the first American atomic bomb detonation was taken by Harold Edgerton.
- Kevlar, the synthetic fiber used in bulletproof vests, was invented by chemist Stephanie Kwolek.
- In 1876, Maria Spelterina was the first woman to ever cross Niagara Falls on a high wire.
- Richard Pavelle solved the Rubik's cube underwater with only five breaths of air.
- As of 2005, there were 37 taxi drivers in New York City named Amarjit Singh.
- Youngest TV host: 6-year-old Luis Tanner, host of TV's *Cooking for Kids With Luis*.
- A Ukrainian monk, Dionysius Exiguus, created the modern-day Christian calendar.
- Russian pilot I. M. Chisov survived a 21,980-foot plunge from an airplane with no parachute. (He landed in three feet of snow, which cushioned his fall.)
- Louise J. Greenfarb of Las Vegas, Nevada, has 35,000 refrigerator magnets. She's been collecting them since the 1970s.

THAT'S MORE DISGUSTING!

• When you sneeze, your body ejects a lot—snot, spit, and pretty much anything else in your mouth and nose—at speeds of up to 100 miles per hour.

• Dung beetles gather poop into apple-size balls, and the females lay their eggs inside. After they hatch, the baby beetles eat their way out of it.

• If your head is chopped off, your brain will keep functioning for about 15 seconds!

• What, exactly, is snot? Mostly water, plus salt and chemicals that help it stay sticky. It may look similar to saliva, but it's not; saliva comes from the salivary glands in your mouth.

• Earwax naturally dries up and forms little balls that drop out when we yawn, chew, or swallow.

• In 1973, folks near Dallas and Boston panicked when slime molds tried to take over their neighborhoods. Slime molds don't move very fast, but they do move.

• Head-shrinking (displaying heads cut off in battle) probably dates back to 200 B.C. or earlier, and was common only in a few tribes in Ecuador, Peru, and Brazil. The Jívaros, a tribe in the Amazon rain forest, used shrunken heads in victory celebrations and feasts—and then discarded them or let the kids use them as toys.

LANDMARKS

- At 555 feet tall, the Washington Monument is the tallest stone building in the world.
- Emperor Shah Jahan of India built the Taj Mahal as a tomb for his wife, Mumtaz Mahal.
- The Grand Coulee Dam in Washington state is the largest concrete structure in the world.
- When it was first built, Egypt's Great Pyramid was 482 feet high, but erosion and settling have shrunk it by about 30 feet.
- When it was first built about 5,000 years ago, England's Stonehenge monument had 30 upright stones. Today, only 16 are still standing.
- The tallest occupied building in Europe is London's Canary Wharf, at 50 stories high.
- Remember the Alamo? The Texas fort was defended by 187 men, all of whom were killed in the battle.
- Armed with sledgehammers, the citizens of East and West Berlin began the destruction of the 26-mile-long Berlin Wall on November 9, 1989. The dismantling was taken over by the government and finished in November 1991.
- The Mason-Dixon line—the imaginary line that separates the northern U.S. from the southern U.S.—is 244 miles long.

THE DEADLIEST SNAKES

Here are nine of the most dangerous snakes in the world.

• **Fierce snake** (Australia): One bite from this killer contains enough venom to slaughter 100 people.

• **Brown snake** (Australia): One drop of its venom—as small as a grain of sand—can kill a human being.

• **Malayan krait** (Southeast Asia): 50% of the Malayan krait's victims die, even if they're treated.

• **Tiger snake** (Australia): This aggressive snake kills more people than any other Australian snake.

• **Saw-scaled viper** (Africa): It kills more people than all other African snakes combined.

• **Boomslang** (Africa): Stand back! The boomslang has very long fangs and can open its mouth to a full 180°.

• **Coral snake** (United States): The coral snake has small fangs, but extremely potent venom. Though it has trouble penetrating clothing, it can easily puncture human skin.

• **Death adder** (Australia): One bite from this snake will paralyze you—and can kill you in six hours.

• **Beaked sea snake** (Asia): It's responsible for more than half of all sea-snake bites. 90% of its victims die.

COOKING GOOD

• To make the perfect boiled egg, make a pinprick in the round end of the shell *before* boiling, so the air can escape. (And be careful—don't crack the egg.)

• Always cook pasta in plenty of boiling water so the pasta can move around as it cooks. That's what prevents it from sticking together.

• Humans are the only creatures on Earth that cook their food.

• Why do onions make you cry? Blame it on the sulfur compounds in the onion—they make your eyes water while you're chopping.

• Anti-crying trick: Stick out your tongue while you're cutting onions. The moisture on your tongue will soak up the onion's airborne chemicals before they hit your eyes.

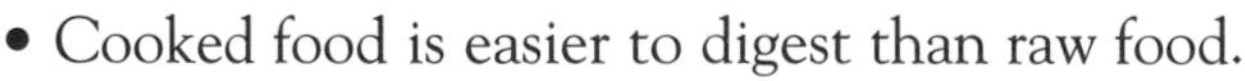

• Cooked food is easier to digest than raw food.

• Why do vegetables get soggy when they're overcooked? The cellulose in their cell walls (which normally keeps them rigid) softens when it's heated.

• What makes food turn golden brown when it's cooked in a frying pan? "Browning" is what happens naturally when the sugar molecules and the amino acids in the food are heated together.

THE CALENDAR

• The ancient Romans were the first to celebrate January 1 as New Year's Day. When? In 153 B.C.

• There was no year 0.

• Luckily, there can never be more than three Friday the 13ths in one year.

• What's the only month that's also a verb? March!

• September 23, 2006, marked the beginning of the year 5767 in the Jewish calendar.

• The Chinese solar calendar is divided into 24 segments of 15 days each. The third month, beginning in early March, is known as the month of the Excited Insects. July is divided into two months known as Slight Heat and Great Heat.

• A year is the amount of time it takes the Earth to orbit the Sun. So, if you're 10 years old, you've traveled around the Sun 10 times! (It's not exactly a year: A year is 365 days—a revolution around the Sun takes 365 days, 5 hours, 48 minutes, and 46 seconds.)

• Brazilians consider August an unlucky month.

• "Kalpa" is a Hindu measurement of time. It's also the world's longest measurement of time—432 billion years.

ANIMALS BY THE NUMBERS

• The oldest cat on record lived to be 34. But one goldfish outlived it, logging in a record life span of 41 years.

• To figure out a dog's age in human years, count the first dog year as 15 years, the second as 10 years, and all the following years as 3 years. So a 6-year-old dog would be: 15+10+3+3+3+3 = 37 human years old.

• An aardvark's tongue is about 17 inches long.

• There are 103 different species of crow.

• An oyster can survive out of water for as long as four months.

• Natural llama hair comes in 22 different colors.

• What a hog: A pig's stomach can hold 32 pints—that's four gallons—of food and drink.

• Ospreys (a.k.a. seahawks) have been clocked at 80 miles per hour.

• Ants can survive underwater for as long as 14 days.

• On a good day, a hummingbird may visit 2,000 flowers before he get his fill of nectar.

• The chickens of the world lay two billion eggs a day, which, by the way, would make an omelet as big as the island of Cyprus—3,500 square miles.

THE WARRIORS

- The word *conquistador* is Spanish for "conqueror."
- The Vikings' favorite weapons? Catapults and battering rams.
- We get the word "vandalism" from the Vandals, a European tribe that completely destroyed Rome in the 5th century A.D.
- 1,200 Japanese kamikaze pilots died sinking 34 American ships during World War II.
- Future president Theodore Roosevelt led a group of soldiers called the Rough Riders (they were mostly cowboys, miners, and law-enforcement officials) in the Spanish-American War.
- The Samurai of Japan wore two swords—one long, one short—and gave them names, believing their swords were the "soul" of their warriorship.
- The Swiss Guard were mercenaries (paid soldiers) who fought in various European armies. Now their only job is to guard the Pope in Vatican City.
- The Spartan boys of ancient Greece were sent to military school at age 6 or 7 and stayed there until they were 20.
- Members of the elite warrior class of the ancient Aztec army were known as "eagle warriors."
- *Ninja* is a Japanese word that means "to do quietly."

HOCKEY TEAM NAMES

Name games that inspired the teams.

• **Anaheim Mighty Ducks**: In 1993, the NHL put a brand-new team in Anaheim, California. It was owned by Disney, which named the team after its 1992 hockey movie, *The Mighty Ducks*.

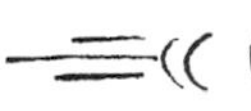

• **Boston Bruins**: The guidelines for a 1920s contest to name the team requested that the name "relate to an untamed animal whose name was synonymous with size, strength, agility, ferocity and cunning; and in the color brown category." Bruin, another name for a brown bear, fit the order.

• **Calgary Flames**: Before they moved to Calgary, the Flames were based in Atlanta, Georgia. They chose their name as a reference to the burning of Atlanta during the Civil War.

• **Detroit Red Wings**: When James Norris bought the team in 1932, he changed their name from the Falcons to honor a team he once played for—the Montreal Winged Wheelers.

• **New Jersey Devils**: Named after the Jersey Devil, a mythical monster that supposedly lives in New Jersey.

FAST FOOD

• Many cultures have their own versions of fast food: In Asia there are noodle shops, in the Middle East there are falafel stands, and ancient Roman cities had bread-and-olive stands.

• One out of every seven Americans eats a diet made up almost *entirely* of fast food.

• 96% of all Americans have been to a McDonald's. Or to put it another way, only 4% of Americans have *never* been to a McDonald's.

• Number of sesame seeds on a Big Mac: 178.

• The British Nutrition Foundation reported that McDonald's Caesar Salad with Chicken Premiere contains 18 grams of fat. A cheeseburger contains only 11.

• Brits eat over 22,000 tons of french fries per week.

• Wendy's introduced the "drive-thru" window in 1972.

• One of Coke's ingredients—called "7x"—is a secret. The few people who know what it is aren't allowed to travel together, in case they all get in an accident.

• Dick and Mac McDonald opened the first McDonald's restaurant in San Bernardino, California, in 1940, selling barbecue.

• First fast food restaurant in North America: White Castle in Topeka, Kansas. They opened in 1921. Hamburgers cost 5¢ each.

SECRET LIVES OF FICTIONAL CHARACTERS

Ever wonder where Kermit the Frog got his name?

• What do Lassie, Rin Tin Tin, Mickey Mouse, Bugs Bunny, Snow White, and Godzilla have in common? They all have stars on Hollywood's Walk of Fame.

• Smoky Bear's original name: "Hot Foot Teddy."

• Mickey Mouse has three fingers and a thumb on each hand.

• In Lima, Peru, there's a tall brass statue of...Winnie the Pooh.

• James Bond debuted in the 1952 novel *Casino Royale*. Since then, he's appeared in 53 books, 23 films, a TV show, and a dozen video games.

• Where did Shrek get his accent? Mike Myers based it on the voice his mother used when she told him bedtime stories.

• Kermit the Frog was named for Kermit Scott, a childhood friend of Muppet creator Jim Henson. The Muppet also delivered the commencement address at New York's Southampton College in 1996.

HAIR ALL OVER

• Studies show that boys' hair grows faster than girls'.

• Fish scales, reptile scales, fingernails, and feathers are made of the same stuff as hair.

• Spiders are hairy all over.

• The hairiest animal in the world is the chinchilla. It has about 60 hairs sprouting from each hair follicle.

• Hair grows faster in warm weather.

• From one strand of hair, scientists can determine what you eat, if you smoke, and your ethnic origin. What they can't tell: your gender.

• In Costa Rica, women decorate their hair with fireflies.

• Any creature with skin or fur can get dandruff, but when animals get it it's called "dander."

• Shirley Temple's hairstyle had exactly 56 curls.

• Crabs are equipped with small hairs on their claws that help them detect vibrations and water currents.

• Leila's Hair Museum in Independence, Missouri, specializes in antique jewelry made of hair.

• A single strand of hair can support 100 grams of weight, about the weight of 20 Hershey Kisses. Based on that, an entire head of hair—about 130,000 hairs—should technically be able to lift two full-grown elephants. (But don't try it.)

LAS VEGAS!

Let's pay a visit to the city that never sleeps.

• The MGM Grand Hotel in Las Vegas washes 15,000 pillowcases every day.

• Every year 100,000 people go to Las Vegas…to get married (230 marriage licenses are issued every day).

• If you wanted to sleep one night in every hotel room in Las Vegas, it would take you 329 years.

• Over 35 million people visit Las Vegas every year. Each of them loses an average of $665 while gambling.

• The most money ever won at a slot machine was $39,713,982.25, at Las Vegas's Excalibur Hotel Casino on March 21, 2003. The winner was a 25-year-old software engineer who had fed the machine about $100 before hitting the jackpot.

• Only 10% of parents who visit Las Vegas bring their kids.

• The Spanish named *Las Vegas*, which means “the meadows,” in the 1800s. The area was an oasis for travelers along the pack-mule trail from New Mexico to California.

• When most people think of Las Vegas, they usually think of “The Strip,” the stretch of glitzy hotels and casinos that was first built in the 1950s. But technically, most of the Strip isn’t in Las Vegas—it’s located in Paradise, Nevada.

• Las Vegas’s biggest wedding chapel is called (what else?) Viva Las Vegas. It seats 100 guests.

• Gangster Bugsy Siegel opened the first hotel in Vegas—the Flamingo—in 1946.

• Over 40,000 people moved to Las Vegas in 2005, bumping up the population to 545,000.

STORMY WEATHER

- There were 27 named tropical storms during the 2005 Atlantic hurricane season, the most active one since record keeping began 150 years ago.
- Sorry, Zorba. Hurricanes are given names starting with letters A through W (no Q, U, X, Y, or Z).
- A hurricane weighs about the same as 40 *million* elephants—more than all the elephants on Earth. Maybe even more than all the elephants *ever* on Earth.
- There are an estimated 16 million thunderstorms globally each year.
- Kampala, Uganda, may hold the world record for thunderstorms: It averages 242 thundery days each year. (Central Florida is pretty stormy too: It has approximately 100 thunderstorm days annually.)
- Thunder is caused by lightning: Air surrounding the lightning heats rapidly, then expands and contracts at supersonic speeds, creating a series of claps and rumbles.
- The coastal deserts of Chile and Antarctica have almost no thunderstorms.
- When is a tropical storm not a tropical storm? When it has wind speeds of more than 74 miles per hour. Then it's a hurricane.

ELEPHANT-ITIS

They're big, they're lovable, and you'd better stay out of their way when they're in a hurry!

• An elephant eats 250 pounds of plants and drinks 50 gallons of water a day.

• An elephant's heart weighs about 48 pounds, a little more than the average six-year-old person's entire body. An entire elephant weighs about the same as 70 grown men.

• The noise that elephants make while digesting food can be heard up to 200 yards away. But they can actually stop the sounds of digestion when they sense danger.

• Is your living room bigger than an elephant? Male elephants are usually about 20 feet long. But don't try to bring one inside: They weigh about 16,500 pounds.

• Elephants have only four teeth for chewing. As their teeth wear down, they're replaced up to six times. Old elephants who've used up all their teeth sometimes starve to death because they can't chew anymore.

• Those ivory tusks are used for defense, digging for water, and lifting things.

• Elephants communicate over vast distances, warning other elephants of danger, telling them where to find water, and signaling that the mating season has begun.

LOTS OF ENERGY

• As long as they're plugged in, appliances like microwave ovens and TV sets use energy even when they're not turned on.

• Turn your computer off when you're not using it; The energy required to keep it in standby mode costs $65 a year.

• Every 60 seconds of every day, thc United States spends almost $1 million on energy.

• Recycling just one aluminum can saves enough energy to run your TV for three hours. Recycling one glass bottle could provide enough energy to light a 100-watt lightbulb for four hours.

• Only 4% of the energy put out by an incandescent lightbulb is light—the rest is wasted producing heat.

• Over its lifetime, the average microwave oven uses more energy running its digital clock than it does heating food.

• Talk about efficient: The Hubble Space Telescope completes one orbit around the Earth in just 97 minutes. To do it, the Hubble uses about the same amount of energy as it takes to light 30 lightbulbs.

OFFICIAL LANGUAGES

• A nation's *official language* is a language that's been given "privileged" status and is used for legal and public documents. Many countries have more than one, especially if several cultural groups live there.

• The country with the most official languages is India, with 23: Assamese, Bengali, Bodo, Dogri, Urdu, English, Gujarati, Hindi, Kannada, Kashmiri, Oriya, Konkani, Maithili, Manipuri, Santhalii, Tamil, Sindh, Telugu, Marathi, Nepali, Punjabi, Malayalam, and Sanskrit. (South Africa is second, with 11.)

• Irish, the *official first* language of the Republic of Ireland, is spoken by less than a third of the population. English, its *official second* language, is spoken by nearly everyone.

• Can a country have *no* official language? Yes—half of the world's nations don't have one, including the United States, the United Kingdom, and Sweden.

• Israel's official languages are Hebrew and Arabic.

• *Sprechen-vous Italiano*? Switzerland has four official languages: German, French, Italian, and Romansch.

• New Zealand's third official language, after English and Maori, is New Zealand Sign Language. It's the first official sign language in the world.

REMARKABLE BODIES

• Sandy Allen, an American, is the world's tallest living woman. She's 7 feet, 7 ¼ inches tall and wears size 22 shoes.

• The shortest man in the world, Younis Edwan of Jordan, is 25 ½ inches tall.

• Bulgaria's Kolyo Tanev Kolev has had a bullet lodged in his skull for more than 60 years.

• In his lifetime, Maurice Creswick of South Africa has donated over 350 pints of blood.

• China's Xie Qiuping has been letting her hair grow since 1973; it's now more than 18 feet long.

• The U.K.'s Garry Turner can stretch his skin a distance of 6 ½ inches.

• Lucky Diamond Rich of Australia had his entire body tattooed with black ink, including his eyelids, the skin between his toes, and his gums.

• Lee Redmond of the United States hasn't cut her fingernails since 1979. Combined, they measure over 24 feet long.

• Weighing in at more than 1,400 pounds, Jon Brower Minnoch of Washington was officially the heaviest person in medical history.

OPEN FOR BUSINESS

- The first Sony product was a rice cooker.
- U-Haul spends more money on advertising in the Yellow Pages than any other company.
- Two-thirds of home-based businesses are owned by women.
- The five most valuable brand names as of 2005: Coca-Cola, Microsoft, IBM, GE, and Intel. The fastest up-and-coming brands are Apple, Blackberry, Google, Amazon.com, and Yahoo!
- Nine out of 10 restaurants fail in their first year. Of the ones that stay open, 9 out of 10 fail in their second year.
- Tuesday is the most productive day of the workweek in Canada.
- Businessmen are called "salarymen" in Japan.
- The average business document is copied 19 times. (And about one in every 10 of them gets lost.)
- Tiffany & Co. made $4.98 in sales on their opening day in 1837.
- The world's most popular perfume: Chanel No. 5. One bottle is sold every 30 seconds.

WEIGHTS AND MEASURES

• How tiny can you get? A "micron" is equal to 1/1000th of a millimeter.

• There's a liquid measure called a "hogshead," probably because it's about the same size as a real hog's head. It holds 432 pints.

• A "dash" is 1/16 of a teaspoon.

• Horses are measured in "hands." This particular kind of hand is equivalent to four inches.

• There are 86,400 seconds in a day.

• A "gross" is one dozen dozens. That's 12 times 12, which equals 144.

• In England, a person's weight is measured in "stones." A stone is equal to 14 pounds, or 6.35 kg.

• A "score" is a unit of measure that means 20. Four score years, for example, is 4 x 20, or 80 years.

• Racetracks are measured in "furlongs." There are eight furlongs in a mile.

• One million hours add up to 114 years.

• Here's an easy way to remember that there are four quarts in a gallon: A quart is a *quarter* of a gallon.

• It takes about 120 drops of water to fill a teaspoon.

MYTHOLOGY

- The Amazon rain forest in South America was named after a mythical tribe of female warriors who supposedly lived there.
- Good name for a running shoe: Nike was the Greek goddess of victory.
- Spiders are called *arachnids* after Arachne, a girl in Greek mythology who wove a tapestry that made fun of the gods and goddesses—not a good idea—so the goddess Athena turned her into a spider.
- The word "cereal" comes from Ceres, the Roman goddess of agriculture and grain.
- Some Native American peoples believed in "tricksters," spirits who took animal forms, such as a fox or coyote, and caused mischief and humiliation.
- In Greek myth, Pandora's box—which contained all the world's evils, and which Pandora was warned not to open, but she did, anyway—wasn't a box. It was a jar.
- The (former) planet Pluto was named after the Roman god of the underworld because it's so far away from the Sun that it seems to be in eternal darkness.
- Wednesday is named for the Norse god Odin. Thursday is named for Thor, the god of thunder.
- The four winds, or *Anemoi*, from Greek mythology had names: They are Boreas (north wind), Notus (south wind), Eurus (east wind), and Zephyrus (west wind).

PENCIL US IN

• The word "pencil" is Latin for "little tail."

• We still call it "lead," but the core of a modern pencil is actually a combination of graphite and clay.

• The amount of carbon in the human body could fill about 9,000 pencils.

• In 1851 there were 319 companies in Great Britain that manufactured pencils.

• Americans buy 2.5 billion pencils a year.

• How many times can a pencil be sharpened? About 17 times.

• 75 percent of all pencils sold in the United States are yellow. Why? Tradition. In the 1800s, the best pencils came from China, where yellow was associated with royalty.

• Three things one ordinary pencil can do: 1) make about 4,000 check marks before needing to be sharpened again, 2) write 45,000 words, and 3) draw a line 35 miles long.

• Pencils are international: They're made of wood from Pacific cedars, graphite from Madagascar, and carnauba wax from Brazil.

• Carpenters use square pencils so they won't roll off roofs.

• The largest pencil ever made is 65 feet high. (It's on the grounds of a pencil factory in Malaysia.)

ANTARCTICA

• Of all the continents, Antarctica is the coldest (with temperatures as low as –129°F), the windiest (with winds as strong as 190 mph), and the highest (with an average altitude of 7,200 feet above sea level).

• Antarctica is the only continent that has never had a native population of humans.

• Some people *visit* Antarctica, though. Summer population: 4,115. Winter population: 1,046.

• Antarctica isn't "owned" by any country. In 1959, 12 nations (including the United States, France, Japan, and the Soviet Union) signed the Antarctic Treaty that set aside the continent for scientific study.

• 90% of all the ice on Earth is located in Antarctica.

• Antarctica has loads of ice, but it gets very little rainfall—only slightly more than the Sahara Desert gets—and doesn't have much snowfall. Technically, that makes this ice-covered continent the largest *desert* on Earth.

• In the winter, the ocean around Antarctica freezes into a vast ice sheet—more than 7 million square miles. The frozen seawater causes deep ocean currents that then drive ocean-current patterns all over the world.

• You might be surprised to know that the South Pole has the clearest, calmest weather of any place on Earth.

IT'S A WILD WORLD

• Octopusses are highly intelligent. One at the Bronx Zoo in New York City figured out how to unscrew the lid from a jar to get to the food inside…in two minutes.

• Black sheep have a better sense of smell than white sheep.

• In one year a single beaver can chomp down more than 200 trees.

• Chickens have terrible night vision.

• A honeybee will die after it stings you—but only if it's a female.

• The next time you see a loaf of bread in the supermarket, think of this: It's larger than a newborn polar-bear cub and about the same weight.

• Millions of years ago, dolphins had legs. They looked like wolves (but acted more like cows).

• One little slug can have as many as 27,000 teeth.

• Sea otters use flat stones and rocks to help them pry mussel shells free from rocks and then open them.

• The clown fish lives among sea anemones, luring in other fish for the sea anemones to eat.

• The three-toed sloth is the slowest mammal in the world, barely reaching 0.1 miles an hour.

AMERICA NUMERICAL

• 45% of Americans don't know that the sun is a star. (Did *you*?)

• Approximately 25% of American kids aged 6 to 14 have a magazine subscription.

• Only 40% of Americans can name more than four of the Ten Commandments.

• Seven out of 10 American homes use candles.

• 80% of American homes have at least one can of WD-40 lubricant.

• 70% of Americans 50 or older say they're "very patriotic." Only 32% of 18- to 34-year-olds say they are.

• 63% of Americans aged 18 to 24 cannot locate Iraq on a map of the Middle East. (Can *you*?)

• Most Americans actually read the nutrition info on food packages, but half of those who *do* say they often purchase items even if they're high in fat or sugar.

• 90% of Americans say they believe in God. (Only 68% believe in the Devil.)

• Eggs-actly two out of five Americans say they eat breakfast every day.

• 22% of the world's beer is produced in the United States.

SPORTS NICKNAMES

• Guys who've been there say that when NFL running back Jerome "The Bus" Bettis crashed into you, it felt like you'd been hit by a bus.

• Eldrick "Tiger" Woods is named after a Vietnamese soldier-friend of his father.

• Teammates called Willie Mays "The Say Hey Kid" because before he knew all their names, he greeted them with "Say hey, man."

• Baseball star Hideki Matsui was a feared hitter even as a kid. He earned the nickname "Godzilla" during Japan's 1992 high school championships.

• Basketball player Karl "The Mailman" Malone got his nickname because "he always delivers."

• All-around athlete and Olympic champ Mildred "Babe" Didrickson Zaharias was named for Babe Ruth after she hit five home runs in a baseball game.

• Hockey's Bernie "Boom-Boom" Geoffrion invented the slapshot. Fans say that his stick hit the puck so hard, it made a booming sound.

• Baseball pitcher Leroy "Satchel" Paige was nicknamed by a friend who was with him on a day when he tried to steal a suitcase.

POST IT

- The United States Postal Service handles over 40% of the world's mail volume.
- The world's largest post office is in Chicago, Illinois; the smallest is in Ochopee, Florida.
- In 1973, the nation of Bhutan issued a set of postage stamps that were tiny phonograph records. They could be played on a turntable and featured folk songs.
- The first stamps didn't have any sticky stuff on the back—you had to paste, pin, or sew the stamp onto the envelope.
- The U.S. Postal Service processes 38 million address changes each year.
- The largest stamp ever printed was issued by China; it measured 8¼ x 2½ inches.
- Any unused U.S. postage stamps issued since 1861 are still valid as postage at their indicated value.
- The Russian space station *Mir* had its own post office.
- A Greek stamp issued in 1954 held the most words ever printed on a stamp: 746.
- Horses, dogs, pigeons, camels, reindeer, and cats have all been used to deliver mail. Only the cat service didn't work out.
- The oldest working post office, in Scotland, has been in operation since 1712.

KNOTS & SKULKS

You know what a group of cows is called: a herd. But what do you call groups of these animals?

- An army of frogs
- A crash of rhinoceroses
- A gang of elks
- An exaltation of larks
- An unkindness of ravens
- A knot of toads
- A sounder of swine
- A mustering of storks
- A bouquet of pheasants
- A skulk of foxes
- A drift of hogs
- A charm of finches
- A clowder of cats
- A shrewdness of apes
- A murmuration of starlings
- A smack of jellyfish
- An ostentation of peacocks
- A sleuth of bears
- A span of mules
- A pace of donkeys

SOUTHPAWS ONLY

Don't read this if you're not a lefty. (Oh, okay, go ahead.)

• At one time in Japan, a husband could divorce his wife if he found out she was left-handed.

• Four of the last six U.S. presidents have been lefties: Gerald Ford, Ronald Reagan, George H.W. Bush, and Bill Clinton.

• In ancient Rome, the left side of the human body was considered evil, and the right side good, so the Latin word for left is *sinister*. The French word for left is *gauche*, which means crude or socially inept. In fact, the word "left" comes from an old English word *lyft*, which means worthless.

• Males outnumber females in left-handedness two to one. And female lefties are much more likely to describe themselves as "tomboys."

• Good news: Lefties make up around 10% of the population but over 20% of Mensa, the high IQ society. Bad news: They also make up more than their share of the populations of prisons and mental institutions.

• Prince Charles and Prince William of England are both southpaws.

THE SEVEN WONDERS OF THE MODERN WORLD

From a list by the American Society of Civil Engineers.

• **The Empire State Building**, completed in 1931, soars 1,250 feet over New York City. It was the world's tallest building until 1972 (the title is now held by the Taipei Financial Center in Taiwan, at 1,671 feet).

• **Itaipu Dam**, built on South America's Parana River by Brazil and Paraguay, is the world's largest hydroelectric power plant. It is actually a series of dams whose length totals nearly five miles. Finished in 1991, it took 16 years to build.

• **The Panama Canal**, a 50-mile man-made waterway across the Isthmus of Panama, took 34 years to build. The amount of digging it required made it the most expensive project in American history up to that time—and the deadliest, too: About 80,000 people died during its construction, mostly from disease.

• **The Channel Tunnel**, also known as the "Chunnel," links France and England. It is 31 miles long, and for 23 of them, it runs 150 feet beneath the seabed of the

English Channel. There are no cars in this tunnel—high-speed trains whiz through its side-by-side tubes.

• **The CN Tower** is the world's tallest freestanding structure, rising about one third of a mile (about 1,815 feet) above Toronto, Canada. A glass floor on the observation deck lets you look down 1,100 feet to the ground. But don't worry—the glass is strong enough to hold 14 hippos!

• **The North Sea Protection Works** was a project nearly as big as the Great Wall of China. The Netherlands is below sea level, so this series of dams and floodgates was built to keep the sea from flooding the country during storms. The biggest part of the project, finished in 1986, was a two-mile-long movable "surge barrier" made of 65 concrete piers, each weighing 18,000 tons.

• **The Golden Gate Bridge**, which connects San Francisco and Marin County, California, was completed in 1937. At 1.2 miles long, it was for many years the world's longest suspension bridge. Experts had thought that winds, ocean currents, and fog would make it impossible to build, but in fact the bridge was built in only four years. The cables that link its two towers are 36.5 inches in diameter—the biggest cables ever made.

BATHROOM NEWS

- Boxer Mike Tyson once owned a house that had 38 bathrooms.

- **Q**: Why are there crescent moons on outhouse doors? **A**: Just like today, public toilets 100 years ago were separated by gender, but because many people back then couldn't read, a half-moon indicated a men's room and a star denoted a ladies room.

- No more fumbling around in the dark—there's a motion-sensitive night-light that flashes a red warning when the toilet seat's been left up, or a green "go" light when the toilet seat is down.

- Greatest distance a toilet has ever been thrown: 23.8 feet.

- Do whales fart? Yes. Survivors of whale farts report that the bubbles are really big and the smell is awful.

- More bad news for swimmers: Blue whales make about 6,000 pounds of poop each day.

- Butterflies don't go to the bathroom.

- Volcanic ash is an ingredient in some toothpastes.

- Consider this fact the next time you have to use a public bathroom—the first stall in the row is most likely the cleanest. That's because it's the least likely to be used.

BASKETBALL TEAM NAMES

How NBA teams got on the ball and found their names.

• **Atlanta Hawks**: They used to be the Tri-City Blackhawks, based in the area of Moline, Illinois; Rock Island, Illinois; and Davenport, Iowa. The team was named in honor of Sauk chief Black Hawk.

• **Denver Nuggets**: The name is a nod to Colorado's 1800s gold mining boom.

• **Detroit Pistons**: Fort Wayne, Indiana, businessman Fred Zollner named the team he owned after Zollner Pistons, his car-parts business. The Fort Wayne Zollner Pistons moved to Detroit in 1957, dropped the "Zollner," and became the Detroit Pistons.

• **Indiana Pacers**: The name comes from another sport: auto racing. A "pacer" is the pace car that starts the state's Indianapolis 500 race.

• **Los Angeles Lakers**: They used to be based in Minneapolis, Minnesota, the "Land of 10,000 Lakes." The team kept the name when it moved to Los Angeles, even though the city has few lakes.

• **New Jersey Nets**: It's not only from a basketball net—it was picked to rhyme with two other New York teams: the New York Mets and the New York Jets.

• **Utah Jazz**: Before moving to Salt Lake City, Utah, the Jazz played in New Orleans, the birthplace of jazz music.

• **Seattle SuperSonics**: When Seattle was awarded a new basketball team in 1967, it was around the time Seattle airplane manufacturer Boeing announced plans to build a high-speed supersonic jet. The plane was never built, but the team took the name "SuperSonics" anyway.

• **Los Angeles Clippers**: The team used to be the San Diego Clippers. The name refers to the tall clipper ships that once traveled in and out of San Diego Bay.

• **New York Knicks**. The team's full name is the New York Knickerbockers. What are knickerbockers? They are pants that are cuffed just below the knee, commonly worn by the 17th-century Dutch settlers who founded New York.

OH, BABY!

• How do they do it? For about six months after birth, infants can breathe and swallow at the same time. (No wonder they burp so much.)

• Shelby Park, born February 10, 2001, was the first baby to have her birth broadcast live on the Internet.

• Glug! Glug! Disposable diapers hold up to seven pounds of liquid.

• The average baby eats 15 pounds of cereal before he or she is one year old.

• An unborn baby's heart beats about 140 times per minute.

• The odds of having quadruplets: about 1 in 729,000.

• In the first few days of life, a baby can see about eight inches away from its face.

• Most new babies have blue eyes because melanin (the brown pigment that colors skin, hair, and eyes) hasn't been fully deposited in their irises or darkened by exposure to ultraviolet light.

• Hey, baby! Try this classic tongue twister: rubber baby buggy bumpers.

• Most American women don't have their first baby until they're at least 24 years old.

• In Japan a baby is born every 25 seconds.

WHAT'S ON TV

- **Q:** What do chimpanzees like to watch on TV? a) talk shows, b) game shows, or c) hockey?
  A: b) Game shows. Researchers are still trying to figure out why.

- On one Japanese extreme game show, a grandmother had to answer questions about pop culture to prevent her grandson from being catapulted into the air by a bungee machine. (She didn't know the answers.)

- Only one out of 10 middle-aged Americans didn't watch TV yesterday.

- A chimp named "J. Fred Muggs" was a regular on the *Today* show from 1953 to 1958. He was also an artist—one of his finger paintings appeared on the cover of *MAD* magazine in 1958.

- 26% of the men and women who watched the 2006 Super Bowl said that watching the commercials was the thing they enjoyed most about the game.

- The first TV commercial, for a wristwatch, ran in 1941. It cost the Bulova Watch Company $9 to air it.

- Since its premiere in 1969, 75 million American kids have watched *Sesame Street.*

- Young adults prefer reality shows, while older viewers like police and medical dramas best.

JAPANESE LANGUAGE

- Japanese is a great language for sound effects. *Gata-gata* is the sound of a chair with one short leg. *Pichiku-pachiku* is the sound of chattering women.
- *Puyo-puyo* is the sound of a blob of gelatin wiggling.
- *Pori pori* is the sound of scratching.
- The Japanese word for "index finger" literally means "person-pointing finger." The ring finger is called the "medicine finger," because it's traditionally used to stir medicine. 
- Ever see a couple where the woman is taller than the man? The Japanese call that *nomi no fuufu*—a flea couple.
- Ringo Starr, the drummer for the Beatles, once appeared on a Japanese advertisement for applesauce. Why? *Ringo* means "apple" in Japanese.
- Japanese cars: Daihatsu Naked, Honda Life Dunk, Honda That's, Mazda Bongo, Mitsubishi Delica Space Gear and Pistachio, Nissan Fairlady Z and Prairie Joy, Rickman Space Ranger, Suzuki Cappuccino, Toyota Deliboy and Toyopet, Volugrafo Bimbo, and Isuzu GIGA 20 Light Dump and Mysterious Utility.

ANIMAL SOUNDS QUIZ

Match the Japanese animal sounds with the animal.

Animal	**Japanese sound**
Dog	Mee-mee
Sheep	Neeow
Duck	Wan-wan
Pig	He-heeh
Cat	Mo-mo
Bird	Qua-qua
Horse	Boo
Cow	Qui-qui

Answer key

Dog: Wan-wan Sheep: Mee-mee Duck: Qua-qua Pig: Boo
Cat: Neeow Bird: Qui-qui Horse: He-heeh Cow: Mo-mo

IN LIVING COLOR

- Most men prefer white bedrooms, but women tend to like blue ones.
- Fast-food restaurants are decorated with lots of yellow, red, and orange—colors thought to stimulate hunger.
- When shopping for casual clothing, most people prefer blue items.
- The ancient Greeks thought they'd have pleasant dreams if they wore white to bed.
- Crayola Crayons currently produces over 120 different crayon colors, but their paper wrappers come in only 18 different colors.
- It was Shakespeare who first called jealousy the "green-eyed monster."
- At one time, people thought that blue would ward off evil spirits. That's why baby boys are dressed in blue. The idea of dressing baby girls in pink came later.
- According to color theory, purple in a child's room will help develop his or her imagination.
- People who sell real estate say that yellow houses sell faster than any other color.
- It's been proven: Blue causes the brain to release hormones that calm people down.

PRECIOUS!

• 34% of the world's gold—about one-third—is mined in South Africa.

• What country uses the most gold? India.

• Approximately 17 tons of gold are used to make wedding rings in the United States every year.

• Diamonds were first discovered over 4,000 years ago in the riverbeds of the Golconda region of India. And until the 1730s, India was the world's only source of diamonds.

• The Hope Diamond is said to be cursed, because it was removed from the eye of a statue of the Hindu goddess Sita.

• Most expensive jeweled egg: The Fabergé "Winter Egg," decorated with more than 3,000 diamonds. In 2002 it was sold for $9.6 million.

• The most expensive perfume, Parfum VI, is packaged in a gold bottle covered with diamonds. Cost: $71,380.

• Carat for carat, emeralds—the traditional birthstone for the month of May—are the most valuable gemstones in the world.

• The world's largest silver nugget was found near Aspen, Colorado, in 1894. It weighed 1,840 pounds!

THE PLANE TRUTH

• The first Boeing passenger plane, the 247, carried only 10 passengers.

• The propeller-driven Black Widow spy plane, designed to give ground troops a quick overview of a particular area, is—surprise!—about the size of your hand.

• The Wright brothers made a total of 105 flights.

• In the United States, there are an average of 240 collisions between airplanes and Canada geese every year.

• On April 18, 2000, 588 military and civilian parachutists from five nations jumped from seven aircraft flying at 12,000 feet over the Santa Cruz Air Base in Rio de Janeiro, Brazil.

• In 2001 an unmanned solar-powered plane called the Helios Prototype achieved the highest altitude ever reached by a propeller-driven aircraft: 96,500 feet, over the island of Kauai.

• There are 13,387 airports in the United States.

• The Airbus A380 is the largest passenger aircraft ever built, with a wingspan of over 261 feet and a length of over 239 feet. It can carry 800 people.

• Iris Peterson, the oldest active flight attendant, is still flying for United Airlines at the age of 85. She was born in 1921 and joined the company in 1944.

(HAVE SOME) CANDY

• Hey, who's eating all the candy? American adults eat 65% of the candy produced worldwide.

• How did Toblerone come up with that triangular shape? They based it on the Matterhorn in the Swiss Alps.

• In some circles, licorice is called "sweet wood" or "Spanish juice."

• The most popular candy in the Netherlands is a salty licorice candy called "Drop" (rhymes with "rope").

• Back in 1953 it took 27 hours to make one Marshmallow Peep; nowadays it takes 6 minutes.

• President Ronald Reagan bought 12 tons of jellybeans during his eight years in office.

• Every year candy manufacturers make 90 million chocolate Easter bunnies.

• When the first 3 Musketeers Bars were introduced in 1932, the package included three small, individual bars—a vanilla, a chocolate, and a strawberry.

• Licorice was found in King Tut's tomb.

• It takes an average of 252 licks to get to the chewy center of a Tootsie Roll Pop.

GORILLAS

• Young gorillas like to play games like Follow the Leader and King of the Mountain.

• Gorillas share 98% of our genes, making them our second-closest relatives (chimpanzees share 99%).

• Gorillas laugh when they're tickled and cry when they're sad or hurt.

• There can be as many as 30 gorillas in a *troop*.

• Every gorilla troop has a leader, a large older male known as a "silverback" because of the gray-silver hair on his back. He makes every decision for the troop—and will protect it to the death.

• Gorillas support their weight on their knuckles when they walk on all fours (unlike monkeys, who use the palms of their hands).

• Adult male gorillas are about 5'6" when they stand up straight.

• Gorillas are mainly vegetarians, although insects make up 1–2% of their diet. They don't seem to drink anything at all—observers think they get their water from the plants they eat.

• The mountain gorilla is an endangered species; fewer than 400 are left in the wild.

TREES

• The world's oldest tree—a bristlecone pine in California called "Methuselah"—is 4,789 years old. Experts say it grows .00035 inches every 24 hours.

• What's the tree most often used in street names? Is it elm? How about maple? Birch? Pine? No—it's oak.

• There are 128 cubic feet in a cord of wood.

• The tallest tree in the world is a coast redwood (*Sequoia sempervirens*) that lives in Humboldt Redwoods State Park, California. It measures about 370 feet high.

• Sri Maha Bodhi, a sacred fig tree in Sri Lanka, is said to be a descendant of the Bodhi tree under which Buddha became enlightened. It was planted in 288 B.C., making it the oldest living human-planted tree in the world.

• *L'Arbre du Ténéré* (the Tree of Ténéré), an acacia tree in the Sahara desert, was once considered the most isolated tree on earth—more than 250 miles away from any other tree.

• The average Christmas tree in an American town square is 12 feet tall.

• "Dogwood" comes from "dagwood"—the tree's slender, strong limbs were perfect for making "dags," that is, daggers.

GOING PLACES

• Half of all journeys taken are less than two miles in distance.

• Around the world in...how many days? The record time by car: 33 days. By bicycle: 78 days.

• Special traffic lanes in the Netherlands are for bicycles only. They even have their own traffic lights.

• In 1870 it took about 29 hours to travel from New York to Chicago. Today it takes less than three.

• How fast does the average escalator travel? About .017 miles per hour.

• Laid end to end, all the roads in the United States would circle the Earth 153 times.

• The most miles ridden backward on a unicycle: 53.

• The average person in Great Britain travels a total of 36 miles by taxi each year.

• A bobsled's top speed is about 90 miles per hour.

• One mile per hour equals 88 feet per minute.

• Things can get so hectic in Hong Kong that delivery times are influenced mostly by traffic conditions on elevators.

• The Japanese travel an average of 1,230 miles by railway per year. The British average 200.

IT'S ABOUT TIME

- A "jiffy" is an actual unit of time: 1/100 of a second.
- If you watch TV for one hour a night between the ages of 6 and 16, you'll have spent 8 months in front of the television.
- How long would it take to type every number from 1 to 1,000,000? It took Marva Drew of Iowa five years.
- The science of timekeeping is called *horology*.
- Back in 1878, Sir Sanford Fleming of Canada figured out that since the Earth rotates once every 24 hours and there are 360 degrees of longitude, there should be 24 worldwide time zones, each spaced 15 degrees of longitude apart. Simple, but brilliant!
- A queen bee lays one egg per minute.
- The part of a sundial that casts the shadow is called a *gnomon*, (pronounced NO-mun). Want to build a sundial? Here's a tip: Use a compass to set the gnomon so it's pointing north-south.
- There are 100 years in a *century*, 10 years in a *decade*, and 5 years in a *quinquennium*.
- Marching in "double time" is 180 steps per minute, "quick time" is 120 steps per minute, and "slow time" is 60 steps per minute.

BIBLE STORIES

• There are more than 750,000 words in the King James Bible.

• The Bible has been translated into 349 languages.

• Southpaws beware: There are 1,600 hostile references to left-handers in the Bible.

• The word "girl" appears only once in the King James Bible. (It's in Joel 3:3.)

• According to folklore, the Adam's apple is a reminder of man's first sin—supposedly it's a piece of the forbidden fruit stuck in the throat.

• How big was Noah's ark? It was 450 feet long, 75 feet wide, and 45 feet tall.

• The Bible contains some pretty long names, but the longest belongs to Isaiah's son: Maher-shalal-hash-baz.

• In the Old Testament there's a giant—a relative of Goliath—who has six fingers on each hand and six toes on each foot.

• *Bibliomancy* is the attempt to tell the future by opening a book (especially the Bible) to a random page and reading the first verse you see.

• Zacharias was struck dumb by God until he agreed to name his son "John." That's the John who later became John the Baptist.

ANTZ

...and not just in your pants.

• There are more than 12,000 species of ants in the world.

• Ants don't just come in black and red—they can also be green, brown, yellow, blue, or purple.

• Most ants are omnivorous—they eat everything... including other insects.

• Queen ants are born with wings. After they fly off to start new colonies, they lose their wings.

• Tropical leafcutter ants are farmers...sort of. They chew leaves to a pulp, then use the decaying leaf pulp to make fungus gardens, which they harvest for food.

• The perfect place for a picnic: There are no ants in Iceland, Greenland, or Antarctica.

• Ants hear with their knees and smell with their antennae.

• The social life of an ant colony is a lot like ours: There are carpenters, farmers, warriors, teachers, hunters, guards, nurses, undertakers, thieves—and even beggars.

• Ants depend on their colony for everything; a lone ant can't survive on its own.

• Scientists think that ants probably evolved from wasps.

NAME POWER

• Some American Indians have two names: a common name and a "power name," which is kept private. Why? Because they believe that anyone who knows the private name can have power over them.

• Children in West Africa are commonly named for the day on which they were born. Monday is Adojoa, Tuesday is Abla, Wednesday is Aku, Thursday is Awo, Friday is Afua, Saturday is Ama, and Sunday is Awushie.

• The Ojibwa people of North America at one time considered it dangerous to speak the names of their own husbands or wives.

• Some Inuit take on new names when they become old, hoping the new name will give them new strength.

• Indonesians may change their names after suffering misfortune or illness. They believe a new name will confuse the evil spirits that brought them grief.

• Ancient Hawaiians thought that names contained *mana*, or power, and that the power in a name could shape a person's character, personality, and destiny.

• Most traditional Jewish families in the U.S. name children after family members who have recently died. The parents hope that the child will have all the virtues of his or her namesake.

RE-USE IT OR LOSE IT

How much do you know about recycling?

- It takes 20 times less energy to make an aluminum can from recycled materials than from new materials… and a can made from recycled materials creates 95% less pollution than a new one does.
- It takes 25% less energy to create paper and glass from recycled materials than from new materials.
- A glass bottle can be recycled an unlimited number of times.
- Every day, American businesses use enough paper to circle the Earth over 20 times.
- Every ton of recycled paper saves 17 trees, 380 gallons of oil, 4,000 kilowatts of energy, and 7,000 gallons of water.
- 84% of all household waste can be recycled.
- Americans recycle less than 15% of their trash.
- *Stannous fluoride*, the cavity fighter found in toothpaste, is made from recycled tin.
- The amount of aluminum that Americans throw out in three months is enough to rebuild 100% of America's commercial airplanes.

MONEY MATTERS

• In 1690 the Massachusetts Bay Colony issued the first paper money in the American colonies.

• A portrait of Sioux chief Running Antelope appeared on the 1899 $5 silver certificate. It's the only time a Native American has appeared on U.S. paper currency.

• The American bison was pictured on a 1901 U.S. dollar, which was nicknamed "the buffalo bill."

• The four main crops of early America—corn, cotton, wheat, and tobacco—all appear on U.S. money.

• The Secret Service was established in 1860. Their original purpose? To combat counterfeiting.

• *E Pluribus Unum*—the motto inscribed on all U.S. coins—was first used in 1795 on the $5 gold piece. It means "one from many."

• First coins produced by the U.S. Mint: 11,178 copper cents in 1793. Value: $111.78, of course.

• The map of Europe portrayed on the 1998 Italian 1,000-lira coin contained four mistakes.

• The only piece of U.S. paper currency to ever have a portrait of a woman was an 1886 $1 silver certificate. The woman: Martha Washington.

• India's State Bank has the most outlets of any bank in the world, with 12,704 locations.

• Check it out: 64% of all retail prices end in the number nine.

• The first known check was written in Europe in the 1650s.

• In 600 B.C. China, one type of coin was called an "ant nose." Why? It was just the right size to plug up dead people's noses—and keep ants out.

• Five-cent coins are called "nickels" because they're made of…you guessed it…nickel. When was a nickel not a nickel? During World War II—they were made with other metals because of nickel shortages.

• Before credit cards became so common, people used to pay for things COD—cash on delivery.

• In 2006 the second-richest man in the world, Warren Buffett, donated two-thirds of his wealth (about $30 billion) to the charitable foundation run by the first-richest man in the world, Bill Gates.

• An easy way to check if you've got a counterfeit bill: Feed it into a vending machine. The government uses magnetic ink; the machine checks for magnetism.

• The word "cash" originally referred to a money box.

• The first credit card, issued in 1950, was a Diners Club card. The man who had the idea in the first place thought it was just a fad and sold his shares in the company for around $200,000.

THE MODERN OLYMPICS

• 1896: 241 athletes from 14 countries participated in the first modern Olympics in Athens, Greece. All of them were male.

• 2004: Athens again, but this time 10,625 athletes (6,296 male and 4,329 female) from 202 countries competed.

• A legendary Hawaiian surfer named Duke Kahanamoku won five medals—three of them gold—for swimming at four different Olympics. In his last Olympics, in 1924, he came in second to Johnny Weissmuller, who went on to star in 12 Tarzan movies.

• The five rings on the Olympic flag represent the five continents that participated in the first modern Games.

• Gymnast Olga Korbut of the Soviet Union was 14 years old when she scored the first perfect 10 in 1976.

• The first modern Olympic Winter Games were held in 1924 in Chamonix (sha-mo-NEE), France.

• The official Olympic motto is *Citius Altius Fortius*. That's Latin for "faster, higher, stronger."

• Lighting the flame at ancient Olympia and relaying the torch to the Olympic stadium was introduced in 1936 at the Berlin Games. The reason: to glorify Hitler's Third Reich.

PALINDROMES

Astounding words and phrases that read the same backward and forward.

- Aha!
- Bob: "Did Anna peep?" Anna: "Did Bob?"
- Toot!
- Dennis, no misfit can act if Simon sinned.
- No, Jon.
- Yo! Bottoms up! U.S. motto, boy!
- Pa's a sap.
- I moan, "Live on, O evil Naomi!"
- Sir, I'm Iris.
- Did Hannah say as Hannah did?
- Dennis sinned.
- Roy, am I mayor?
- Enid and Edna dine.
- Harass selfless Sarah.
- Delia and Edna ailed.
- Ah, Satan sees Natasha.
- Dennis and Edna sinned.
- Won't lovers revolt now?
- Yawn a more Roman way.
- Nurse, I spy gypsies. Run!
- Max, I stay away at six a.m.
- Did Dean aid Diana? Ed did.
- Revenge, my baby Meg? Never!
- Oh, who was it I saw? Oh, who?

SING A SONG

• "Twinkle, Twinkle, Little Star," "Baa, Baa, Black Sheep," and "The Alphabet Song" all have the same melody—originally from a French folk song.

• Popular country singer Dolly Parton released her first record, "Puppy Love," on March 20, 1959. She was 13 years old.

• When Congolese musician Fidele Babindamana performed in France with the stage name "Fidele Zizi," everyone laughed. Why? In French, "Fidele Zizi" means "faithful wee-wee."

• Elvis Presley's manager, Colonel Tom Parker, was quite a wheeler-dealer. In addition to grabbing an estimated 50% to 75% of Elvis's income, he sold both "I Love Elvis" and "I Hate Elvis" buttons.

• Paul McCartney's "Yesterday," voted the most popular song of the 20th century, was originally called "Scrambled Eggs." The opening line: "Scrambled eggs / Oh baby, how I love your legs."

• "Happy Birthday" was the first song ever performed in outer space. The *Apollo IX* astronauts sang it on March 8, 1969.

• "Over the Rainbow," the song Judy Garland sings in *The Wizard of Oz*, was ranked #1 on the American Film Institute's list of the 100 Greatest Songs in American Films.

I'LL DRINK TO THAT

Bottoms up! Here are some fascinating facts about the world's favorite beverages.

• Early soft drinks came in bottles. What was the first soda in a can? Clicquot Club ginger ale, in 1938.

• Every year, Dunkin' Donuts serves an estimated 650 million cups of coffee.

• Some experimental versions of 7UP, sold outside the United States: 7UP Mint, 7UP Raspberry, and 7UP Ice (which left a cool sensation in the mouth).

• Budweiser beer is named for a town in the Czech Republic.

• Pepsi central: Pikeville, Kentucky (population 6,500) consumes the most Pepsi per capita of any American city.

• In what country do people drink the most coffee per day? Norway.

• Australians gulp down an average of 25 gallons of soda per person every year.

• Ground-up acorns were used as a coffee substitute during the Civil War.

EARTHQUAKE!

• Sounds weird, but it's true: A magnitude 6.0 earthquake is 10 times greater than a 5.0 earthquake.

• 500,000 earthquakes occur in the world every year. Humans can feel only about 100,000 of them, and of those only 100 cause damage to buildings or property.

• In a 2001 experiment to see if they could create an earthquake, one million British schoolchildren jumped up and down in unison for a minute. (It didn't work.)

• Where was the strongest earthquake in American history? Probably not where you'd think. It took place in Tennessee in the winter of 1811. The quake created tidal waves on the Mississippi River and caused church bells to ring in Boston, Massachusetts…almost 1,000 miles away.

• Florida and North Dakota have the fewest earthquakes in the U.S.; Alaska has the most—as many as 4,000 a year.

• The deadliest earthquake on record—estimated at 8.0 on the Richter scale—killed approximately 830,000 people in China in 1556.

• There are more than 1,500 earthquakes a year in Japan.

• A few days before an earthquake destroyed the ancient city of Helice in 373 B.C., worms, snakes, and weasels abandoned the city for safer ground.

FISHY STORIES

• The largest ocean carnivore is the sperm whale. Adult males can grow up to 60 feet long and weigh 80,000 pounds.

• When you think of a starfish, you think of a creature with 5 arms—but a basket starfish can have 50 arms or even more!

• Count 'em: A lobster has 10 legs.

• Sperm whales eat about a ton of food a day. Their favorite? Squid.

• Jellyfish have been around for a very long time. They appeared in the oceans about 650 million years ago, *before the dinosaurs*.

• Sea horses lay up to 400 eggs at a time.

• Giant tube worms can grow up to eight feet long. They live inside hard, protective, shell-like tubes that attach to rocks.

• Home Sweet Home: In order to mate and lay eggs, sea turtles will migrate thousands of miles to return to the same beach where they hatched.

• Look! A giant squid's eye measures 15 inches across.

• How big are blue whales? Picture a whale that's as long as three Greyhound buses and weighs as much as 30 elephants. That's big.

• A shrimp's heart is located in its head.

• A sperm whale's largest teeth are an awesome 11 inches long—roughly as long as a human's forearm.

• The bodies of jellyfish are made up of 95% water. They have no bones or cartilage, no hearts or blood, and no brains.

• A dolphin sleeps with one half of its brain at a time, and with one eye closed.

• Orcas, the largest members of the dolphin family, have the second-largest brains in the animal kingdom. Who's got the *largest*? The sperm whale—with a brain that can weigh in at 20 pounds.

• The world's deepest-dwelling fish, *Abyssobrotula galatheae*, was found near Puerto Rico at a depth of 8,372 meters—that's more than five miles down! Its eyes are virtually nonexistent. (Since it's so dark at that depth, eyes have become unnecessary and useless.)

AVERAGE AMERICANS

• The average American watches 28 hours of TV each week.

• The average American spends 27 minutes per day reading the newspaper and 17 minutes reading books.

• The average American home contains six radios.

• The average American opens the refrigerator 22 times a day.

• On average, Americans spend $1,300 on utility bills each year.

• While shopping for groceries in a supermarket, the average American will make 14 impulse purchases. Examples: chewing gum, cold soda, cookies, tabloid newspapers, an eyeglass-repair kit, lottery tickets, or anything marked "*NEW!*"

• In an average year, an average American will spend five times longer in their car than they'll spend on vacation.

• The average American kid scarfs down 46 slices of pizza per year.

• Here's a scary thought: The average American will develop a phobia by the age of 13.

KIDS AT WORK

Before the 1920s—in the days before child-labor laws and compulsory education—most children worked. How would you like to have had one of these jobs?

• You've seen *Mary Poppins*, so you know what a chimney sweep does—clean chimneys. But many chimney sweeps were small children, six to eight years old, who had to crawl up chimneys and loosen the soot with a broom.

• Gillie boys helped fishermen by baiting hooks, pulling nets, and preparing food.

• A loblolly boy was an assistant to a ship's doctor. One of his responsibilities was to feed the patients, and what he fed them was a thick oatmeal or porridge called *loblolly*.

• Office boys worked—you guessed it—in offices. What did they do? Sharpened pencils, swept floors, stuffed envelopes, and ran errands.

• Being a powder monkey might sound like fun, but it was a dangerous job. The powder in question: gunpowder. Kids carried it to the cannons during battles.

• Children often worked as vendors, selling things on city streets. Besides newspaper boys, there were "hot corn girls," who sold corn on the cob for a penny.

EVERYBODY'S BODY

• Your nose gets runny when you cry because the tears from your eyes drain into your sinuses…and dribble out of your nose. (Eww!)

• Even if you ate while standing on your head, the food would still end up in your stomach.

• Travelers beware: Flying frequently across several time zones can shrink your brain.

• It seems there's a name for *everything*: The food that's digested in your stomach is called *chyme*.

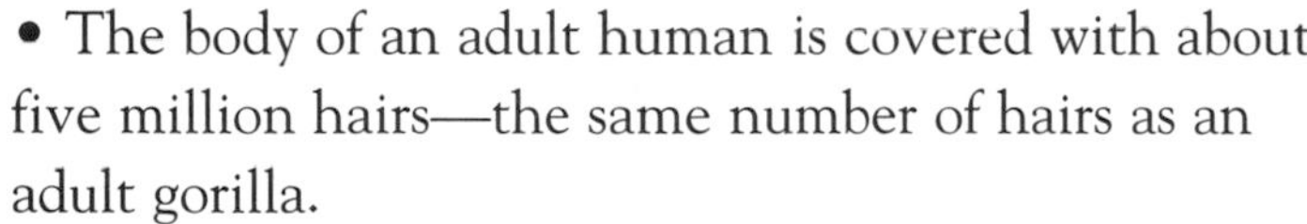

• The body of an adult human is covered with about five million hairs—the same number of hairs as an adult gorilla.

• Your empty stomach has a capacity of less than two ounces. But when you start to fill it, your tummy can expand to hold a quart (about four juice boxes).

• Onion or garlic breath comes from the lungs, not the mouth: The odor-causing components get into your blood, and when the blood reaches your lungs you breathe out smelly gas. (Eww!)

• Breathing normally, you suck air into your nose at 4 mph. A sneeze shoots out of your nose at 100 mph.

• If you're right-handed, you sweat more under your left arm. If you're left-handed, you sweat more under your right arm.

• Sleeping on your right side helps gas escape more easily from your stomach. So, here's the good news: you can burp while you snore.

• Your stomach lining contains millions of tiny glands that produce *hydrochloric acid*. This acid is so strong that it can dissolve metal.

• There are 639 named muscles in the human body.

• The average fart contains several different gases, including nitrogen (59%) and methane (7%).

• If you pluck a hair from your head (or someone else's head), it will take 56 days—almost two months—for it to reappear.

• Move your hand. You just used 35 muscles.

• Bile produced by the liver is what makes your poop a brownish-green color. (Eww!)

• About 50% of the bacteria in your mouth live on the surface of your tongue.

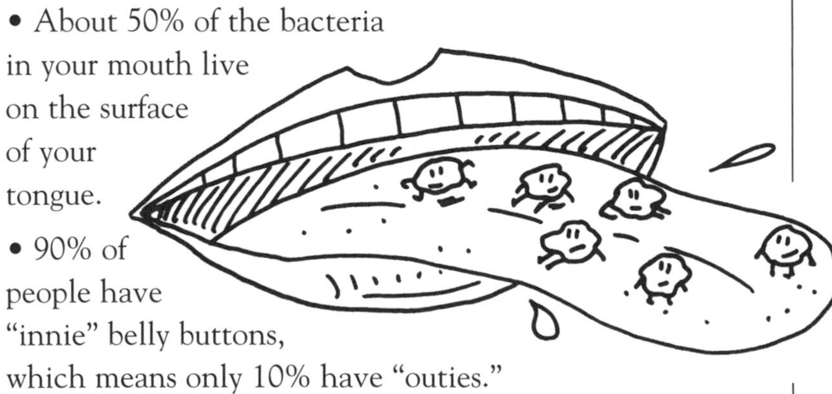

• 90% of people have "innie" belly buttons, which means only 10% have "outies."

HORSING AROUND

• Argentinian cowboys, called *gauchos*, have over 200 words to describe the color of horses.

• The oldest known horse lived to 62 years old.

• The average horse secretes (yuck!) nine gallons of saliva a day.

• Hair from a horse's mane or tail is used in making paintbrushes and violin bows.

• Car models named for horses: Colt, Bronco, Mustang, Pinto.

• A horse has 205 bones.

• The first cloned horse was born in Italy in 2003; the mare that gave birth to her was her identical twin.

• The word "equestrian" comes from *equus*, Latin for "horse."

• Who's the only athlete to appear simultaneously on the cover of *Time*, *Newsweek*, and *Sports Illustrated*? The racehorse Secretariat. In 1973 he won the Triple Crown of horseracing: the Kentucky Derby, the Preakness, and the Belmont Stakes.

• The cowboy slang word for horse—cayuse—comes from the name of a Native American tribe.

EXTREME WORLD

• The largest living thing in the world is an underground fungus in Oregon. It covers about 2,000 acres.

• The oldest organism on Earth: a colony of bacteria that had been entombed in sea salt in New Mexico for 250 million years. Scientists discovered it in 2000.

• By using a nearby fossil of an identical plant, scientists estimated the age of a King's Holly plant found in the rain forests of Tasmania at over 43,000 years old.

• The oldest living animal: a Madagascar radiated tortoise presented to the royal family of Tonga by British captain James Cook in the 1770s. It lived to an estimated age of 188.

• The hottest place on Earth: the El Azizia desert in North Africa. On September 13, 1922, the temperature was officially measured at 136°F, but scientists believe it may have actually reached 150° in some areas.

• Manta rays can grow up to 19 feet long and weigh as much as 2,300 pounds.

• *Extreme* height: Astronauts grow as much as three inches taller in space. Engineers have to factor it in when designing space capsules and uniforms.

• In parts of the Atacama Desert in Chile, it has never rained. Ever.

EDUCATION

• Boulder, Colorado, is the most educated city in America—more than half of the adult residents have college degrees.

• The oldest school in the United States is New York's Collegiate School, founded in 1628.

• The first library was established by the Greeks in 530 B.C.

• Hawaii's Lahainaluna High School was the first school established west of the Rocky Mountains. It was founded in Lahaina, Maui, in 1831, when Lahaina was a busy whaling port.

• Maria Montessori opened the first Montessori school in Rome, Italy, for the children of poor families.

• Utah's Brigham Young University offers more than 100 ballroom dancing classes a year.

• In the 10th century, the Grand Vizier of Persia, Abdul Kassam Ismael, carried his complete library with him wherever he traveled. It required more than 400 camels to carry all 117,000 volumes.

• In 2004, Kimani Maruge of Kenya finally got his chance to go to elementary school…at 85 years old.

FOREIGN TONGUE TWISTERS

Dutch: *Vissers die vissen naar vissen en vissers die vissen die vangen vaak bot. De vissen waar de vissende vissers naar vissen, vinden vissers die vissen vervelend en rot!*

English translation: "Fishermen that go fishing for fish and fishermen who fish often catch flounders. The fish that the fishing fishermen fish for, find fishermen that go fishing annoying and beastly!"

French: *Le poivre fait fièvre à la pauvre pieuvre.*

English translation: "The pepper gives the poor octopus fever."

Hawaiian: *Hele wawai o ka malamalama, ka malamalama, o ka malamalama, hele wawai o ka malamalama, ka malamalama o ke Akua.*

English translation: "I am walking in the light, in the light, in the light, I am walking in the light, in the light of God."

Latin: *Te tero Roma manu nuda date tela latete.*

English translation: "I'll crush you, Rome, with my bare hands."

Italian: *Trentatré Trentini entrarono a Trento, tutti e trentatré, trotterellando.*

English translation: "Thirty-three Trentonians came into Trento, all thirty-three trotting."

Japanese: *Kaeru pyoko-pyoko mi pyoko-pyoko awasete pyoko-pyoko mu pyoko-pyoko.*

English translation: "Take two sets of three frog croaks. Add them together and they make six frog croaks."

Zulu: *Amaxoxo ayaxokozela exoxa ngoxamu exhibeni.*

English translation: "The frogs are talking loudly about the monitor lizard."

HEY, DADDY-O!

Some animals have pretty cool dads.

• A father sea catfish keeps the eggs of his young in his mouth until they're ready to hatch. He won't eat a thing until the babies are born, which can take weeks.

• After a mother wolf gives birth to pups, the father guards the den. As the pups grow, he plays with them and teaches them how to live in the wild.

• Rheas are large South American birds similar to ostriches. From eggs to chicks, the father rhea feeds, defends, and protects his young until they can survive on their own.

• The male Darwin frog hatches the female's eggs in his mouth. He eats and continues his normal frog life until the tadpoles become tiny frogs and jump out.

• The male red fox will bury food near the den to train his pups to sniff and forage, and he'll play ambush games with them to teach them self-defense.

• When a Siamese fighting fish mom lays her eggs, the dad catches them in his mouth and drops them into a nest he's prepared. He stands (or swims) guard over the nest, too.

• A cockroach dad eats bird droppings to obtain precious nitrogen that he carries back to feed his young.

MYTHICAL CREATURES

• According to legend, the Abominable Snowman has four toes on each foot.

• In almost every seafaring culture there have been reports of mermaid sightings. Even Christopher Columbus said he'd seen one.

• Don't blink! According to legend, if you've captured a leprechaun you cannot take your eyes off him…or he'll vanish.

• There's a round-the-clock webcam now trained on the lake where the Loch Ness Monster supposedly lives. (No one's seen the creature yet.)

• Chinese dragons—especially yellow ones—are considered to represent good fortune.

• A dragon is often portrayed as guarding an object or an area. Makes sense: The word "dragon" comes from the Greek *draconta*, which means "to watch."

• Greek mythology has a lot of monsters: griffins (part eagle, part lion), the Hydra (a nine-headed serpent), Cerberus (the three-headed hound who guards the entrance to Hades), the one-eyed Cyclops, and the three Gorgons (female monsters who had sharp fangs and hair of living, venomous snakes), to name a few.

ON THE MAP

Every state has something to brag about (including the fact that you live there).

• Arkansas has the only active diamond mine in the United States.

• The only royal palace in the United States, Iolani Palace, is in Hawaii. Its last occupant, Queen Liliuokalani, was forced to surrender Hawaii to the American government in 1893.

• The washing machine was invented in Newton, Iowa, in 1884…which is why Newton is the washing machine capital of the world.

• The world's largest ball of twine is 40 feet around and weighs more than 17,000 pounds. It stands inside its own shrine in Cawker City, Kansas.

• New Mexico has an official state question: "Red or green?" The answer refers to types of chili peppers.

• Maine is the only state whose name is one syllable.

• Shoes were first sold as left-and-right pairs in 1884 at Phil Gilbert's Shoe Parlor in Vicksburg, Mississippi. Before that, everybody just bought two shoes that were exactly the same.

• Ahlgrim's Funeral Home in Palatine, Illinois, has a miniature golf course in the basement. You need to call for a reservation to play.

ECOLOGY

• The word "ecology" means "study of the house," from the Greek *eco* for house or dwelling place.

• How would they do it? A group of NASA engineers and American astronomers believe that moving Earth into a new orbit would solve the problem of global warming—or at least add another 6 billion years to its life.

• Rain forests cover only 7% of the Earth's surface, but they contain more than half the plant and animal species on the planet.

• In 2006 Alaska's Iditarod dogsled race had to be moved 30 miles north—the usual location wasn't cold enough (because of global warming).

• There are still undiscovered species in the rain forests, but experts fear that they might become extinct before they're found and recorded.

• Almost 70% of the Earth is water, but only 1% is usable: 97% is in the ocean and 2% is frozen.

• In a typical day, humans destroy 115 square miles of tropical rain forest, create 72 square miles of desert, eliminate between 40 and 100 species, erode 71 tons of topsoil, and increase their population by 263,000.

• 40% of the pure water in your house gets flushed down the toilet.

FOOTBALL TEAM NAMES

Name games that inspired the teams.

• **Arizona Cardinals**: The original 1901 team wore hand-me-down jerseys from the University of Chicago. They were red, like a cardinal.

• **Baltimore Ravens**: Named after a poem by Baltimore's native son, Edgar Allan Poe: "The Raven."

• **Chicago Bears**: When the Decatur Staleys moved to Chicago in 1921, they had to share Wrigley Field with a Major League Baseball team—the Cubs. With that in mind, the team changed its name to the Bears.

• **Green Bay Packers**: It was the first football team to receive sponsorship. In 1919, the Indian Packing Company gave the team $500 for uniforms and equipment.

• **Philadelphia Eagles**: When the team joined the National Football League in 1933, the country was recovering from the Great Depression. The Blue Eagle symbol used in President Franklin Roosevelt's National Recovery program inspired the Eagles' name and logo.

• **Kansas City Chiefs**: After being lured out of Texas by Kansas City mayor H. Roe "Chief" Bartle, the Dallas Texans changed their name to the Chiefs.

WATCH THE BIRDIES

• It's common for a mockingbird to know 25 to 30 songs. Although most songbirds learn their songs before they're one year old, a mockingbird keeps learning new tunes its whole life.

• Real airheads: If you've ever wondered if woodpeckers get headaches from all that hammering, the answer is no. Pockets of air in their heads act as cushions for their brains.

• Albatrosses can travel thousands of miles each flight, landing only every few years to breed. Luckily for them, they're able to sleep while they fly.

• The hummingbird is the only bird that can hover and fly in any direction: up, down, forward, or backward.

• In some cultures, cuckoos are considered omens of a happy marriage.

• Lovebirds are small parrots that mate for life—that's why it's so important that they're kept in pairs in captivity.

• Ever wonder how many feathers there are in a peacock's beautiful tail display? Around 200.

• Flying in a V formation helps birds conserve energy: It reduces wind resistance, and when the lead bird gets tired, another bird takes over.

SCRABBLE

This word-based board game is one of the most popular of all time. Ever played it?

• Scrabble is sold in 121 countries around the world and has been translated into 29 different languages.

• If you played the word QUARTZY as your first word in a game, it could be worth 126 points.

• Top Scrabble players know as many as 14,000 words —about seven times as many words in the average vocabulary—but they don't necessarily know the meanings.

• There are 109 permissible two-letter words in American Scrabble, from AA (a kind of lava) to ZO (a kind of cattle).

• The highest recorded score in a game of Scrabble was 1,049, by Phil Appleby in 1989.

• The highest score in a single turn was 392; the word was CAZIQUES (native chiefs of the West Indies).

• There are 15 O's in an Italian Scrabble set, but no J's, K's, W's, X's, or Y's.

• In the English version of Scrabble, the letter Q is worth 10 points. In Portuguese, it's worth 6.

• In the Finnish version of Scrabble, the letter D is worth 7 points, but it gets only 2 points in English.

THE SEVEN NATURAL WONDERS OF THE WORLD

• **The Grand Canyon** was created by millions of years of wind and water erosion from the Colorado River. The rocks of the canyon walls range in age from 250 million years old at the top to more than 2 billion years old at the bottom.

• **Paricutín volcano** erupted out of a Mexican cornfield on February 20, 1943. Located just outside the city of Michoacán, about 200 miles west of Mexico City, Paricutín grew to 10,400 feet in just nine years, making it the fastest-growing volcano in recorded history. Its lava destroyed two villages and hundreds of homes, but caused no fatalities.

• **The harbor of Rio de Janeiro**, in what is now Brazil, was first seen by Portuguese explorers on January 1, 1502. The Portuguese thought they had reached the mouth of an immense river and named their find River of January—Rio de Janeiro. The spectacular harbor's landmarks include Sugarloaf Mountain and Corcovado Peak.

• **The northern lights**, also called the aurora borealis,

occur when solar particles from the sun collide with gases in the Earth's atmosphere. The energy created by the collision is emitted as photons (light particles). The many collisions produce an aurora—lights that seem to dance across the sky.

• **Victoria Falls**, the world's largest waterfall, lies on the border between Zambia and Zimbabwe in Africa, where the Zambezi River suddenly plummets 420 feet over a cliff. The first white man to see it, in 1855, was a Scottish missionary named David Livingstone. Although he named it after the Queen of England, native Africans continue to call it *Mosi-oa-Tunya*, which means The Smoke That Thunders, because the water makes thunderous clouds of spray as it falls.

• **The Himalayas**, the highest mountain range in the world, was created about 60 million years ago. India (at that time a separate continent) rapidly moved northward and collided with Asia, and the crash produced these amazing mountains. The famous Mt. Everest stands above the other peaks at 29,035 feet, making it the tallest mountain on the planet. Thousands of people have tried to climb it; more than 700 have succeeded, but at least 150 have died trying.

• **The Great Barrier Reef**, located in the Coral Sea off the coast of Queensland, Australia, is the world's largest coral reef. It is over 1,400 miles in length—so long that it can be seen from space. An estimated 1,500 species of fish and 350 types of coral live and grow on the Great Barrier Reef.

MILESTONES IN HISTORY

• The Chinese invented sunglasses in the 1400s. The first people to wear them were judges who were trying to conceal their expressions in court.

• The presidential mansion was originally gray. It wasn't called the White House until it was painted white to cover the damage caused by the British in the War of 1812.

• Squanto, one of the first Native Americans the Pilgrims met in the New World, had lived in England for nine years. He'd been taken from his village by around 1605 and eventually made his way back home.

• The flag that Francis Scott Key was looking at off in the distance when he wrote "The Star-Spangled Banner" was 30 feet high by 42 feet wide.

• It makes for a great story, but Thomas Crapper did not invent the flush toilet. The first patent was awarded to Joseph Adamson in 1853.

• If you'd been born before the ninth century, you wouldn't have had to study punctuation. There wasn't any!

• Painted fingernails originated in China; the color indicated social rank.

SPIDERS

• Spiders spin silk out of organs called "spinnerets."

• Spiders can get trapped in their own webs if they trip or fall.

• The "dragline silk" that spiders use to get down from the ceiling to the floor is comparatively stronger than a steel rope.

• The idea of farming spiders for their silk doesn't work very well because they tend to eat each other.

• Some spiders walk up walls by secreting sticky silk onto their feet. Others use microscopic hairs on their legs that slip into the wall's nooks and crannies.

• The full name of the spider-heroine of *Charlotte's Web* is Charlotte A. Cavatica, after the scientific name of the barn spider: *Araneus cavaticus*.

• The world's biggest spider, the Goliath birdeater tarantula, hardly ever eats birds. It prefers rodents and frogs.

• Camel spiders are the world's fastest: They've been clocked at close to 10 miles per hour.

• Genetic engineers have bred goats that have spider-silk genes inside them. Silk proteins can be harvested from the goats' milk.

• Spiders aren't insects—they're *arachnids*. Unlike insects, they have no antennae and they have eight legs (insects have six legs).

THE ROYALS

• King Philip IV of Spain (1605–1665) is rumored to have smiled only three times in his life.

• Queen Elizabeth I of England (1533–1603) owned 150 wigs and 2,000 pairs of gloves. She wore a necklace with a perfume bottle attached—probably because the people around her smelled bad. (Elizabethans believed that taking baths could make you sick.)

• In 2005, Swaziland's King Mswati III bought 10 new BMWs for his wives.

• Number of serfs that Empress Catherine the Great of Russia (1729–1796) gave away as gifts: 45,000.

• Ethelred the Unready became king of England in 968 A.D., at the age of 10. He was called "Unready" because he had trouble making decisions.

• Eighteen French kings have been named Louis. Louis IX became a saint; Louis XVI died on the guillotine.

• When Chinese emperor Qin Shi Huang died in 210 B.C., more than 8,000 life-size statues were buried in his grave with him.

• King Charles VIII of France (1470–1498) had six toes on one foot.

LADIES & GENTLEMEN

• In the United States, there are about five million more women than men.

• The average woman walks at a pace of 274 feet per minute. The average man walks faster, but not by much: He moves at 275 feet per minute.

• In 1950 only 2% of the members of the armed forces was female. As of 2004—54 years later—the number was up to 15%.

• Women have more sweat glands than men, but men's sweat glands are more active (they sweat more).

• Men talk on their wireless phones more than women, but women use their camera phones more than men.

• Women are more likely to have gardened in the last 12 months: More than half of all women got dirt under their fingernails. Only a third of all men did.

• Who reads more? Women. Last year 55% of women opened a book, while only 38% of men did.

• Is this fair? In 2003, females aged 15 and older working full-time all year earned 76¢ for every $1 their male counterparts earned. In 2004, that was up to a whopping…77¢.

GEOGRAPHY

• Old news from the Middle East: Damascus, Syria, was a flourishing city a few thousand years before Rome was founded in 753 B.C., which makes it the oldest continuously inhabited city in the world.

• The name Canada is from a Huron-Iroquoian word meaning "village" or "settlement."

• The country with the smallest population: Pitcairn Island in Polynesia, with 67 residents.

• Only 20 of Ohio's 2,500 lakes are natural—all the rest are man-made.

• Brazil got its name from the nut, not the other way around.

• The northernmost point in the United States is Point Barrow, Alaska; the southernmost point is more than 3,600 miles away in Ka Lae, Hawaii.

• There are no arid deserts in Europe.

• Amatignak Island, Alaska, is the westernmost point in the United States. Believe it or not, 70 miles *west* of that is the *easternmost* point: Pochnoi Point on Semisopochnoi Island, Alaska. (It's on the other side of the international date line, where the eastern hemisphere begins.)

• Pop quiz: Is Australia an island or a continent? Answer: Scientists are still arguing about it.

HOUSE PETS

• Only 22% of people say they would sacrifice themselves to save their husband or wife. But 85% say they would risk their life to save their pet.

• Babies who live with cats and dogs tend to develop fewer allergies.

• According to a survey of pet owners, 21% of dogs and 7% of cats snore.

• Nine out of 10 pet owners think of their pets as members of the family.

• Iguanas recognize their human owners and greet them differently than they greet strangers.

• A family paid Texas A&M University $2,300,000 to clone their pet Collie, Missy.

• If you want to move to Hawaii, your cat or dog might have to be kept in quarantine there for as long four months. If your dog is part wolf, forget about him moving there at all.

• It's official: After studying thousands of papers on the subject, the National Academy of Sciences has declared that too many pets are overweight.

• 10% of women who own cats say they have ended a relationship because their partner didn't like their cat.

AMERICAN HISTORY

- Among the names the early Congress considered for their newly independent country were: United States of Columbia, Appalachia, Alleghania, and Freedonia.
- President George Washington made sure his six horses had their teeth brushed every day.
- America's first bank, the Bank of North America, was established in Philadelphia in 1781.
- The first woman to run for U.S. president: Victoria Woodhull, in 1872. (She lost to Ulysses S. Grant.)
- There were 11 states in the Confederacy, 23 states in the Union.
- 102 Pilgrims sailed to America on the Mayflower in 1620. Fewer than half survived the first winter.
- Patrick Henry owned 65 slaves when he threw down the challenge "Give me liberty or give me death."
- July 4th didn't become a legal holiday until 1941.
- Annapolis, Maryland, served as the capital of America from 1783 to 1784.
- President Ulysses S. Grant once got a speeding ticket for riding his horse too fast. The fine? $20.

EVOLUTIONARY, WATSON!

• Trilobites, ancient relatives of shrimp, spiders, and insects, were the first creatures on Earth to have eyes.

• The most common fossil animals are brachiopods, a type of shellfish.

• It used to be thought that the smallest dinosaur was the compsognathus, which was about the size of a chicken, but the fossil of a smaller one, the microraptor, was recently found in China. It's about the size of a crow.

• The first shellfish made their appearance about 570 million years ago.

• The first plant known to grow on land, the *Cooksonia*—named after Australian scientist Isabel Cookson—had no roots, leaves, or flowers.

• Magnolias are the first known flowering plants.

• 450 million years ago, the Sahara desert was covered in ice.

• 200 million years ago, Antarctica was near the equator and joined to Africa, Australia, India, and the tip of South America.

• Neanderthals were named for the valley (the *thal*) where they were discovered in 1856: the Neander Valley in Germany.

THE WRITTEN WORD

• Bram Stoker's *Dracula* has been translated into 44 languages.

• Wow! Writer Tom Wolfe used 2,343 exclamation points in his novel *Bonfire of the Vanities.*

• Watch your language: Shakespeare used the word "damned" 105 times in his plays. (But don't *you* use it!)

• There are only 17 syllables in the Japanese poetry form called *haiku*. Most haiku focus on the beauty of nature, but the form is open to wordplay like this:

After the warm rain
the sweet smell of camellias.
Did you wipe your feet?

• *Where the Wild Things Are* author Maurice Sendak named his dog "Herman" after Herman Melville, the author of *Moby Dick.*

• The monster in Mary Wollenstonecraft Shelley's book *Frankenstein* doesn't die at the end of the story like he does in the movies. He's last seen running across an Arctic ice field.

• British author Charles Dickens wrote *Little Dorritt* based on his own life experience: He had to go to work when he was only 12 years old because his father was put into debtor's prison.

BEASTLY APPETITES

- The only mammals who feed exclusively on blood: vampire bats.
- Electrifying fact: Carnivorous animals (meat eaters) won't eat an animal that's been hit by lightning.
- A baby robin eats 14 feet of earthworms every day.
- The Yanomami Indians of South America call jaguars "The Eaters of Souls," because of the legendary belief that they consume the spirits of the dead.
- The anaconda snake's teeth aren't for chewing. They hold onto prey so it can't escape.
- Tigers have a reputation as man-eaters, but usually it's only old or injured tigers who attack humans. Why? They have trouble keeping up with their usual prey.
- Rabbits love licorice (but don't feed them candy!).
- Swimming along the surface of the water, an archer fish can shoot water out of its mouth to knock down flying bugs.
- The polar bear has an enormous appetite—it can eat as much as 100 pounds of whale blubber in a single sitting.
- Dromedary camels (one-hump camels) can drink 30 gallons of water in 10 minutes.

SUPERSTITIONS

• You won't find a fourth floor in a Japanese hospital, because the Japanese word for "four" sounds a lot like the Japanese word for "death."

• Scandinavian superstition: A boy and girl who eat from the same loaf of bread are bound to fall in love.

• Some people think it's bad luck to put a hat on a bed or put shoes on a table.

• Chinese folks clean their homes from top to bottom *before* New Year's Day. Cleaning *on* New Year's Day might sweep away good fortune.

• In folklore, owls are notorious prophets of doom: A hooting owl is thought to be giving a warning of death.

• In some parts of England, rum is used to wash a baby's head for good luck.

• A common good-luck custom in Spain is to eat one grape per second for the last 12 seconds of every year. (Eat small grapes…or you might choke, and there goes your good luck.)

• Don't sing Christmas carols out of season. It's bad luck.

OLD-TIME OCCUPATIONS

- Men who collected and sold secondhand clothes were called *ragpickers*.
- Animals used to be the main means of transportation, and they can be pretty messy. So one of the jobs of a *carter* was to remove animal poop from the streets.
- A *fuller* was a person who cleaned dirty clothes.
- *Peddlers*, riding horses laden with pots, pans, needles, and cutlery, traveled through villages and towns trading their goods for other products offered by local people.
- From at least 3000 B.C., when few people knew how to write, *scribes* held important positions at temples and palaces because they could write and record information.
- The *tinker* traveled from door to door on horseback, carrying his tools in his saddlebags. His jobs included plugging holes in leaky basins, making handles for iron dippers, and fixing spoons and bowls.
- Every village had a *town crier* who announced the important news of the day.
- Medieval *viziers* listened to problems and impartially decided who was right and who was wrong. The vizier of yesterday is what we'd call a judge today.

• 13th-century *wandering minstrels* were street entertainers who hoped to be rewarded with money by onlookers.

• *Coachmen* transported wealthy people in comfortable, closed, four-wheeled carriages pulled by one or more horses.

• *Cotters* were hired by wealthy landowners to work on farms at harvest time, dig ditches, plant crops, and thatch roofs.

• In the old days, *doorkeepers* didn't just guard the entrances to temples and private homes—they were also responsible for guarding the sheep at night.

• The main job of *apothecaries* was to grind minerals, vegetable oils, and animal fats to make medicines, cosmetics, and perfumes.

• People who carry your bags—porters and bellmen—were once known as *baggage smashers*.

PENGUINS

• Penguins do not live in the Arctic, the region around the North Pole. Penguins live only in the southern hemisphere.

• Emperor Penguin Fact #1: Unlike most bird species, it is the male Emperor penguin, not the female, who hatches the eggs.

• Emperor Penguin Fact #2: A father Emperor penguin will withstand the Antarctic cold for 60 days or longer to protect his egg, which rest on his feet covered with a feathered flap.

• Emperor Penguin Fact #3: During this entire time the papa penguin doesn't eat a thing. Most lose about 25 pounds while they wait for their babies to hatch.

• Emperor Penguin Fact #4: The fathers feed the chicks a special liquid from their throats. When the moms finally return to care for the young, the dads head for the sea to eat…and rest.

WINNING WORDS

The words that turned ordinary school kids (well, maybe not so ordinary) into winners of the National Spelling Bee.

- 2006: **Ursprache** (*noun*), a parent language, especially one reconstructed from the evidence of later languages
- 2005: **Appoggiatura** (*noun*), in music, an embellishing note, usually one step above or below the note it precedes and indicated by a small note or special sign
- 2004: **Autochthonous** (*adjective*), aboriginal, indigenous, native
- 2003: **Pococurante** (*adjective*), indifferent, apathetic; (*noun*) one who does not care
- 2002: **Prospicience** (*noun*), seeing ahead, knowing in advance, foreseeing
- 2001: **Succedaneum** (*noun*), something that can be used as a substitute (especially any medicine that may be taken in place of another)
- 2000: **Démarche** (*noun*), course of action, maneuver
- 1999: **Logorrhea** (*noun*), excessive talkativeness, especially when the words are uncontrolled or incoherent, as is seen in certain psychiatric illnesses
- 1998: **Chiaroscurist** (*noun*), an artist who uses light and shade in painting or drawing

WORDS OF WAR

• Napoleon was only 26 years old when he led the French Army to a successful invasion of Italy. His last battle was at Waterloo, which he lost—that's why when someone loses, we say they "met their Waterloo."

• The United States produced 41,500 Sherman tanks during World War II. Today, Russia has more tanks than the United States: 21,000 to the U.S.'s 16,000. China comes in third, with 11,000.

• For the birds: Thirty-two pigeons won Dickin Medals (awarded to honor the work of animals in war) for carrying secret messages during World War II.

• The Battle of Palmito Ranch, in the far south of Texas, was the last land battle of the Civil War. The Confederates won that battle, but within a month, all their land forces had surrendered to the North.

• In 1989 the U.S. military purchased 5,118,470 pairs of green socks.

• Elastic waistbands in pants were first used during World War II—the metal used in zippers was needed for making weapons and aircraft.

• Since the founding of the United Nations in 1945 (in response to World War II), more people have been killed in wars than during World War II itself.

• In the months after Iraq's 1990 invasion of Kuwait, the U.S. Army bought 25,550 bottles of sunblock.

ROBOTS

• A machine qualifies as a robot if it can a) get information from its surroundings and b) do something physical, like manipulate objects.

• Nine out of 10 robots that exist today work in factories—more than half make automobiles.

• Some robots "see" using ultrasonic sound, like bats do. But for a robot to have depth perception, it needs stereoscopic vision (two eyes) like ours.

• The robot Robug III explores places where extreme radiation would kill a human.

• In need of some underwater exploration? Sounds like a job for MIT's RoboTuna.

• The Mini-Andros is a robot programmed to locate and dispose of bombs.

• Experts say that by 2010, robots will have the intelligence of a lizard.

• By 2020, robots will be as intelligent as mice, and they'll be able to learn on the job.

• The 2030 robot will be as smart as a monkey.

• Aaah! By 2040, scientists expect robots to be as intelligent, competent, and creative as humans.

PLANT YOU NOW, DIG YOU LATER

• Does Barbra Streisand smell better than former first lady Barbara Bush? Horticultural experts say yes, judging by the scents of the roses named after them.

• The substance in poison ivy that makes you itch is an oil called *urushiol*.

• Botany Bulletin: It's possible to grow bananas in Iceland, in soil heated by underground hot springs.

• The trunk of the African baobab tree can reach a circumference of 180 feet.

• Average life span of a city tree: about eight years. (The same tree would live 20 to 50 years in the wild.)

• An olive tree can live for 1,500 years.

• What's in a name? The Venus *flytrap* feeds primarily on ants—not flies.

• Builders used 3,994 oak trees to construct Windsor Castle in England.

• As many as 179 species of tree can be found in a 2.5-acre area of rain forest.

• Where does vanilla come from? From a bean—the fruit of an orchid vine that is native to Mexico.

• There's a rose named for Whoopi Goldberg.

ANIMAL ODDS & ENDS

• Some scientists believe that cuttlefish communicate by changing their color.

• Most orcas in captivity die before they reach their early 20s; in the wild they can live 80 years or more.

• Where there's a weigh: 250 hedgehogs = 1 lion.

• The Sumatran tiger has the most stripes of any tiger species; the Siberian tiger has the fewest.

• Baby birds have an "egg tooth"—a notch on the front of their beaks—that helps them peck out of the egg. The egg tooth falls off after they've hatched.

• Lions are the only cats that have a tuft on the end of their tails.

• A tiger's paw prints are called "pugmarks."

• The life span of a black rhinoceros is 30 to 35 years in the wild and 35 to 45 years, or even more, in captivity.

• One bird sings lots of different songs about different things: food, a nest, flying, or pretty much anything.

• The elephants that helped Hannibal's army cross the Alps in 218 B.C. had platforms on their backs that carried four soldiers each.

• A cow can produce nearly 50 gallons of saliva a day.

• The chicken is the closest living relative of the Tyrannosaurus rex.

• Lions and tigers and…oh, my! A "liger" has a lion father and a tiger mother; a "tigon" has a tiger father and a lion mother.

• Don't feed your cat milk—most adult cats are lactose intolerant, and drinking milk will give them diarrhea.

SPACE TRAVELERS

• Sputnik I, the first artificial satellite in space, weighed 185 pounds.

• At liftoff, the U.S. Space Shuttle weighs about 4.5 million pounds.

• No one knows why, but the Moon smells like exploded firecrackers and, therefore, moondust smells like gunpowder.

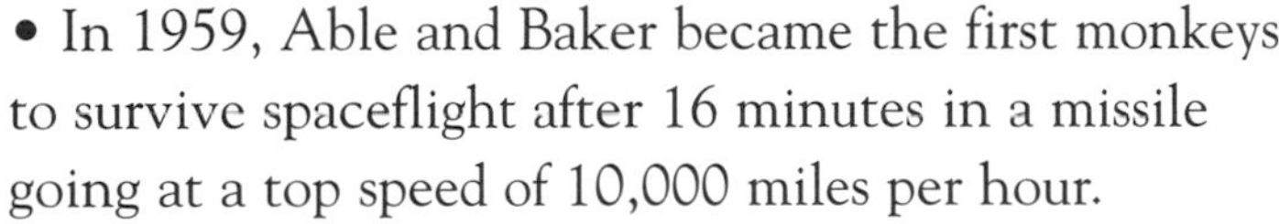

• In 1959, Able and Baker became the first monkeys to survive spaceflight after 16 minutes in a missile going at a top speed of 10,000 miles per hour.

• If you want to imagine the dramatic view of Earth that the Apollo astronauts had from the Moon, visualize the sky turning utterly black—while the Sun continues to shine brilliantly.

• Because there's no wind or water on the Moon, the footprints left by the Apollo astronauts will not disappear for at least 10 million years.

• Techno-trivia: The technology used in one Game Boy in the year 2000 was more advanced than all the computer power used to put the first man on the Moon.

• Alan Shepard was the first American astronaut, and he flew only 116 miles into space on that first trip.

• Neil Armstrong, the first person to walk on the Moon, spent only 152 minutes there.

ON SAFARI

- Rhino horns are made of compacted hair.
- The only animal that's a danger to an adult gorilla—aside from humans—is a leopard. But the two animals rarely mess with each other.
- Hippopotamuses kill more people in Africa than any other wild animal does.
- Here's how African buffaloes decide which direction to move: Individuals face the direction they want to go, and when enough of them are facing one particular way, the entire herd takes off in that direction.
- The good old days: Herds of springbok antelope were once the largest in the world, containing more than 10 million animals and covering an area 100 miles long and 15 miles wide.
- Scientists are still trying to figure out why only one dominant female in a colony of naked mole rats produces eggs, and why the other females don't start to produce eggs until she dies. (By the way, they're not really naked, they just don't have very much hair.)
- Almost human: Older chimpanzees teach their youngsters how to use tools like sticks to extract termites from their nests, rocks to crack open nuts, and leaves to clean themselves.

LIFE IN JAPAN

• In Japan, people dial 110 in an emergency, not 911.

• Calpis is a popular yogurt-flavored soft drink in Japan, though to English speakers, the name sounds like something you might find in the corner of a barn.

• More funny drink names: Pocari Sweat (sports drink), Mr. BM (canned coffee), Sourpis (another yogurt-flavored drink).

• In Japan, the trains are so crowded that the station employees sometimes have to p-u-u-u-u-sh the passengers inside. And they wear white gloves to do it.

• Japanese people wash their hands and feet before going to bed.

• In public restrooms, modest Japanese women used to flush the toilets several times to cover the sound of their activities. So now many stalls have recorded "flushing" sound effects to conserve water.

• Public restrooms in Japan don't have paper towels. Everyone carries handkerchiefs around instead.

• Most Japanese homes have combination sink-toilets. When you flush, water flows out of a faucet and into the tank so you can wash your hands as the tank fills.

• Westerners see a man in the moon. Japanese see two rabbits making rice cakes.

• When Japanese people see a hearse drive by, they hide their thumbs to protect their fathers. That's because the word for thumb is literally "parent finger."

• In Japan, the first dream of the new year is considered very important. If you dream of an eagle, an eggplant, or Mt. Fuji, it will be a good year.

• 25 billion pairs of chopsticks are sold every year—about 200 pairs per person.

• Japanese people wash themselves before they get into the bathtub. (The bathroom floor has a drain.)

• Western people point to their chest when talking about themselves, but Japanese people point to their nose. The Japanese character for "me" is a combination of the characters for "nose" and "rice."

• Japanese taxis have remote-control back doors that the drivers can open without getting out of their seats.

• In Japan, store clerks hand you your change on a tray lined with what looks like Astroturf. That makes the coins easier to grab.

HISTORY QUIZ

• **Q**: How long was the Pony Express in operation?

A: Based on Hollywood movies, most people believe it was around for years. Wrong. The Pony Express was in operation only from April 1860 to November 1861. (It was put out of business by the telegraph and the transcontinental railroad.)

• **Q**: Who was the first president of the United States?

A: George Washington? A few historians actually consider *John Hanson* to be the first U.S. president. As the presiding officer of Congress under the Articles of Confederation (a precursor to the Constitution), Hanson's official title was "President of the United States in Congress Assembled." And everyone—including George Washington—called him "Mr. President."

• **Q**: Was Albert Einstein ever considered a candidate for the presidency of Israel?

A: On November 18, 1952, Israeli officials asked the world's most famous scientist to become president of Israel. Einstein declined, saying he was too old (he was 73) and that he lacked the "natural aptitude and the experience to deal properly with people."

• **Q**: Who founded the Boy Scouts?

A: In 1908, a secret agent for the British Military, Robert Baden-Powell, started the Boy Scout movement.

MUSICAL MISCELLANY

• In England, an eighth-note is called a *quaver*. A 64th-note is called a *hemidemisemiquaver*. Now, hang onto your hat: A 128th-note is called a *semi-hemidemisemiquaver* or *quasihemidemisemiquaver*.

• On a 1907 visit to Brandenburg, Germany, it took England's chubby King Edward VII so long to squeeze into his ceremonial uniform that the band had to play his national anthem 17 times—a world record.

• Qatar has the shortest national anthem of any country; it can be sung in 32 seconds.

• It would take 120 hours to listen to all the music composed by Beethoven, 175 to listen to Bach's, and 240 hours—that's 10 full days—to listen to Mozart's.

• The average American listens to recorded music for about 45 minutes a day.

• At a recent soccer match between teams from China and Greece, each team stood respectfully, thinking a song on the loudspeaker was the other team's national anthem. What were they really listening to? A toothpaste commercial.

• Most people know that a piano has 88 keys, but most do not know that a harp has 47 strings.

• Greece's national anthem has 158 verses.

MORE ABOUT EARTH

- The tallest iceberg measured 550 feet above the water level.
- Earth is 4.55 billion years old (give or take 10 million).
- Air temperature goes down about 3.5°F for every 1,000 feet you go up in altitude.
- Fifty of the 221 volcanoes in the Philippines are active.
- About half the Sun's radiation is absorbed by the Earth's surface. (The rest bounces back into the atmosphere.)
- In November 1992, a thunderstorm was reported on St. Paul Island, Alaska—the first one there in 40 years.
- Earth's northernmost point—the geographic North Pole—is in the Arctic Ocean. The northernmost point on land is Kaffeklubben Island, east of Greenland.
- How many colors in a rainbow? As many colors as you can see; all the colors of the rainbow are there.
- The pull of gravity on Earth is six times stronger than it is on the Moon.

LIGHTNING

• At any given moment there are 2,000 thunderstorms happening in the world. Lightning strikes somewhere 100 times every second.

• Lightning causes an average of 93 deaths and 300 injuries in the United States each year.

• The Empire State Building was designed to be a lightning rod…and it sure is: It's struck by lightning about 100 times each year.

• Your chances of being struck by lightning are only one in 600,000, but those chances go up if you live in Florida, the lightning capital of America.

• The safest place to be during a thunderstorm is in a building with a lightning rod. Next safest: a car with the windows rolled up, *as long as you don't touch any metal parts*.

• If lightning strikes a car, the metal body will conduct the charge into the ground. The car's rubber wheels offer *no* protection, and rubber soles on your shoes won't protect you either.

• Scared of lightning? Avoid open spaces, including fields, ballparks (location of 28% of lightning deaths and 29% of injuries), and shelter under trees (18% of deaths, 13% of injuries).

• Lightning's not all bad: It puts nitrogen into the soil, which plants need to survive.

MORE REPTILES

• There are lizards with very small legs or no legs that look like snakes. You can tell the difference because most lizards have movable eyelids.

• Snakes have 200 to 400 segments in their backbone; humans have 32 to 34.

• Crocodiles' nostrils are on top of their heads, so they can breathe while the rest of their bodies are underwater. Some alligators can survive all winter with their heads frozen in ice and their noses out to breathe.

• Gila monsters can survive for months without food.

• Here's how a snake "smells": Its forked tongue collects chemicals from the air, which it then pulls in and holds against the "Jacobsen's organ" in the roof of its mouth.

• There are more than 7,000 reptile species on Earth.

• Chameleons change color according to their mood, not to blend into their surroundings.

• Lizards, tortoises, and salamanders move like fish, by swishing their bodies from side to side. The movement compresses first one lung and then the other, so they can't run fast and breathe deeply at the same time. That's why lizards run in short bursts—they have to stop to catch their breath.

WEIRD WORLD HOLIDAYS

• Mexico's Cinco de Mayo is not an independence day celebration. It commemorates an 1862 military victory over the French.

• In China, September 20th is "Love Your Teeth Day."

• In Italy, Santa Claus is called *Babbo Natale* (Daddy Christmas). In Russia, he's *Ded Moroz* (Grandfather Frost), and Norway has a Christmas gnome called *Julenissen.*

• In 1605, Guy Fawkes tried to blow up the British Parliament. Even though he was executed for the crime, the British gave Fawkes a holiday—he was "the only man ever to enter Parliament with honest intentions." Every November 5th, Guy Fawkes Day is celebrated with bonfires and fireworks.

• At the beginning of every February, Japanese communities gather at temples to celebrate the Bean Throwing Festival. Evil spirits are driven away by hurling beans into the crowd.

• The Chinese Dragon Boat Festival is an ancient event celebrating the poet Chu Yuan, who drowned in 277 B.C. Dragon-shaped boats race each other while fans throw rice and bamboo leaves into the water.

THAT'S THE MOST DISGUSTING...

- The Romans used crushed mouse brains as toothpaste.

- Strange but true: Picking your nose is good for you— the inside of your nose stays cleaner. Bonus: Swallowing dry snot strengthens your immune system.

- When Eskimo babies have colds, their mothers suck the snot out of their noses.

- Which is cleaner, spit or pee? The urine: it's sterile.

- The longest tapeworm ever found inside the human body was 35 meters long, or about 115 feet. Picture a worm 11 stories high…

- According to studies, every year, 14 bugs find their way into your mouth while you sleep. And, yes, you do swallow most of them.

- How much snot does the average person produce each day? About one quart. How much snot does the average person swallow each day? About one quart.

- How Frogs Throw Up: **Step 1)** The frog "tosses" its stomach, so the stomach is dangling out of its mouth. **Step 2)** The frog uses its forearms to dig out all the stomach contents. After that it swallows the nice clean stomach back down again.

FAMILY TIES

- The average American family is 3.14 people.
- Until 1993, the names of all French children had to be chosen from an official list.
- There are more children in India working to support their families than in any other country in the world.
- Why? Why? The average four-year-old child asks more than 400 questions a day.
- Almost one in three families in the United States and France has a dog.
- Assam tribespeople of Africa call their families *maharis*, meaning "motherhoods."
- A penny saved: The typical American family has about $3,800 in the bank.
- Younger brothers and sisters in Nigerian families refer to their older siblings as "Senior Brother" or "Senior Sister."
- The odds of having quadruplets are 1 in 729,000.
- On Tomb Sweeping Day, Chinese families visit the gravesites of family members to worship their ancestors and clean and repair the tombs.
- The average American family of four spends more than $13,000 on medical expenses in a year.
- Your first cousin's daughter isn't your second cousin—she's is your first cousin, once removed.

IT'S A CORNY WORLD

Corn shows up in the most amazing places.

• Without corn, frozen pizza would be a soggy mess. Cornstarch protects the crust from soaking up the sauce like a sponge.

• Corn keeps wallpaper from sticking to the wall too quickly. Cornstarch in the glue slows down the stickiness of the paper, giving wallpaper hangers time to arrange each strip in the right place.

• Corn syrup prevents lollipops from dripping.

• There's corn in chalk and crayons: Cornstarch is used as a binder to keep them from falling apart in your hands.

• Every tiny ridge in a corrugated cardboard box is glued down with cornstarch. (No wonder cockroaches like to eat cardboard.)

• Some blankets are woven with corn fibers, and some pillows and comforters are stuffed with corn fill.

• There are biodegradable plastic bags made from cornstarch.

• Some disposable diapers contain cornstarch. (It helps the plastic break down.)

ANIMAL GEOGRAPHY

• More than a million caribou live in Alaska...outnumbering the state's humans by nearly two to one.

• Belize is the only country in the world that has a jaguar preserve.

• Anacondas live in the swamps and rivers of the dense forests of South America, but they also live on the island of Trinidad.

• The sandgrouse is a bird native to Africa's Kalahari Desert. When a pair nests, every day the male flies up to 50 miles away to soak himself in water, so that on his return his chicks can drink from his feathers.

• The largest congregation of vertebrates (animals with backbones) ever recorded was a colony of Brazilian free-tailed bats that numbered over 20 million individuals.

• In Africa, droughts are common. Luckily for elephants, the oldest dominant female of the herd is likely to remember where water could be found during the last drought—and how to get there.

• Every Spring, thousands of European starlings (a kind of bird) gather at sunset over the marshes of western Denmark and fly together in a massive circular formation known as a "Black Sun."

• Prairie dogs are native to North America west of the Mississippi. But they aren't dogs at all—they're rodents.

• The Florida Everglades is the only place in the world where both alligators and crocodiles live in the same environment.

• Half of the world's chameleon species live in Madagascar.

• The pronghorn, which is *not* an antelope, is the last surviving member of the family *Antilocapridae*, antelope-like mammals that lived exclusively in North America.

TONGUE TWISTERS

• She stood on the balcony, inexplicably mimicking him hiccupping, and amicably welcoming him home.

• Imagine an imaginary menagerie manager imagining managing an imaginary menagerie.

• While we were walking, we were watching window washers wash Washington's windows with warm washing water.

• A big black bug bit a big black bear, made the big black bear bleed blood.

• On mules we find two legs behind and two we find before. We stand behind before we find what those behind be for.

• Suddenly swerving, seven small swans swam silently southward, seeing six swift sailboats sailing sedately seaward.

• A tutor who tooted the flute, tried to tutor two tooters to toot. Said the two to the tutor, "Is it harder to toot or to tutor two tooters to toot?"

• I'm not a smart feller, I'm a smart feller's son and I'll keep feeling smart till the smart feller comes.

• Silly Sally swiftly shooed seven silly sheep; the seven silly sheep Silly Sally shooed shilly-shallied south.

ODDS & ENDS

• If Wal-Mart were a country, it would rank about 20th on a list of the most productive countries in the world.

• Ireland's official national emblem isn't the shamrock—it's the harp.

• The leading cause of poisoning for children under the age of six is liquid dish soap.

• Shore thing! Four out of five Californians live within 30 miles of the coast.

• Researchers have calculated the ideal number of people needed to create a colony in space: 160—about the size of a small village.

• 18% of the people who died in 2000 did so as a result of smoking and tobacco; 16% died because of poor diet and lack of exercise.

• The world's first theme park was Santa Claus Land, which opened in 1946 in Santa Claus, Indiana—nine years before Disneyland opened in California.

• Clean fact: One end of a soap molecule attracts water, the other attracts oil (a.k.a. greasy dirt).

• Because there's no R, Y, C, S, or T in Hawaiian, "Merry Christmas" is "Mele Kalikimaka."

• The name "Illinois" comes from a Native American word meaning "tribe of superior men."

• In 2004 an Alaskan chicken farmer injected eggs with dye. Result: orange, red, green, purple, pink, and blue chicks.

• Eco-fact: A dishwasher uses 25 gallons of water per load; a washing machine uses 30 gallons per load.

• Blast off! It takes eight minutes for the Space Shuttle to accelerate to its top speed—more than 17,000 mph.

• The biggest bottle of wine may be bigger than you: The 4½-foot tall "Maximus," produced by Beringer Vineyards in California, holds 173 bottles of red wine.

• The number 2,520 can be divided by 1, 2, 3, 4, 5, 6, 7, 8, 9, and 10, with no fractional leftover.

• Flower power: During Japan's War of Dynasty in 1357, warriors wore yellow chrysanthemums as a pledge of courage.

• There are 63 patterns of dots in the braille writing system.

• Barney (the purple dinosaur) is from Dallas, Texas.

• There are 2,500,000 rivets in the Eiffel Tower.

• Paper or plastic? It turns out that making plastic bags uses less energy and produces less waste than making paper bags. (But plastic doesn't decompose.)

• Only 42% of London's transit system—called the London Underground—is actually underground.

• Ever heard an elephant joke? Here are two:

Q: How do you fit four elephants into a Volkswagen?
A: Two in the front and two in the back.

Q: How do you fit five elephants into a Volkswagen?
A: Two in the front, two in the back, and one in the glove compartment.

• The bestselling Crayola crayon box is the set of 24 colors.

• Arrrgh! The nursery rhyme "Sing a Song of Sixpence" originated as a coded message used by pirates; Blackbeard, for example, paid his sailors sixpence a day plus a serving of rye whiskey.

TEMPERATURES

- What is "room temperature" exactly? There's nothing exact about it—it's somewhere between 68°F and 73°F.
- The freezing point of water is 32°F (0°C), and the boiling point is 212°F (100°C).
- –40° Fahrenheit is the same temperature as –40° Celsius, and vice versa. But that's the only temperature that the two scales have in common.
- 98.6°F is the normal core body temperature of a healthy, resting adult.
- The Sun's outer visible layer has a temperature of about 10,000°F. Its core can get as hot as 22.5 million degrees Fahrenheit.
- Butter melts at 88°F.
- Hypothermia begins when body temperature goes below 95°F. The condition becomes critical at 90°F.
- Hyperthermia—when the body produces or absorbs more heat than it can deal with naturally—occurs above 104°F.
- Paper burns at 451°F.
- The temperature of molten lava is about 2,000°F.
- Refrigerators should be kept below 41°F—but above 32°F so the food doesn't freeze.
- The temperature on the Moon varies from –387°F at night to 253°F during the day.

HELPFUL HINTS

• If you encounter a shark, remember that its top speed is 42 mph, so don't try to outswim it. Just swim as calmly as you can toward shore.

• If you're sending flowers to someone in Russia, make sure there's an odd number of blossoms in the bunch. Bouquets with an even number of flowers are for funerals only.

• Should you happen to find yourself in the grip of a crocodile's jaws, push your thumbs into the croc's eyeballs—it will let you go instantly.

• Apples are a natural remedy for diarrhea.

• Do not smile at any dog that you feel may be dangerous. To the dog you'll appear to be baring your teeth—a sign of aggression.

• When you've moved to a new location, unpack your computer and let it come to room temperature before you start hitting those keys.

• Freckle tip: According to some sources, you can lighten freckles by rubbing them with fresh-cut eggplant every day. You should see a difference in a week or so.

• Do you have dry hair? Try this natural and easy recipe for a moisturizing shampoo: Add two tablespoons of olive oil or one egg to a cup of baby shampoo.

ACTING HUMAN

• Here's something to think about: The human brain produces about 70,000 thoughts a day.

• Ha! The average person laughs 15 times a day.

• How many senses do humans have? Your basic five senses are touch, taste, sight, smell, and hearing. But some scientists say we actually have nine senses: the basic five, plus balance, heat, pain, and body awareness. What do you think?

• On average, men blink about 6.2 million times per year. Women blink about 12 million times.

• There are six facial expressions that are universal: happiness, sadness, disgust, fear, anger, and surprise.

• The most frequently used facial movement? A smile.

• Women smile more than men, but children smile more than adults.

• Remember this the next time you stub your toe: Scientists say that laughter reduces pain.

• Do you sneeze when you step out into a bright sunny day? It's called a "photic sneeze," and about one out of three people do it.

• In times of extreme stress, humans can sometimes perform amazing feats of strength. For example, in 1982, Angela Cavallo lifted a Chevy Impala to free her teenage son, who was trapped underneath it.

YOU BUG ME

- There are more than 1,800 species of fleas.
- The average butterfly cocoon contains more than 1,000 feet of silk.
- The practice of eating insects has a name: *entomophagy*. People in many cultures have been eating insects for centuries (and plenty still do).
- Most lipsticks—and even some fruit drinks—are colored red with a dye from an insect known as the cochineal.
- It's a bird! It's a bat! It's…an atlas moth. Atlas moths are so big, they're sometimes mistaken for medium-sized bats.
- If you lined them up end to end, all the earthworms under a typical football field would stretch for 94 miles.
- Some fleas freeze at night and thaw out—still alive—the next morning.
- Bees have to fly a total of 72,000 miles to gather enough honey for one jar.
- A tiny fly called a "midge" beats its wings 62,000 times a minute.
- There are 45 species of ladybug in Great Britain and 450 in North America.

MORE WACKY TOWN NAMES

• Tarzana, California, is where Edgar Rice Burroughs lived when he wrote jungle adventure stories featuring a main character called...Tarzan.

• Ding Dong, Texas, is in Bell County.

• Peculiar, Missouri, was named by the postmaster after the town fathers told him, "We don't care what you name it as long as it's sort of peculiar."

• Lake Webster in Massachusetts is called "Webster" because no one can pronounce its real name: Lake Chargoggagoggmanchauggagoggchaubunagungamaugg.

• Halfway between Pine, Oregon, and Cornucopia, Oregon, is the town of...Halfway.

• People in Gnaw Bone, Indiana, tell colorful stories of how the town got its name, but the truth is that it's named after the French city of Narbonne.

• The town of Chicken, Alaska, was going to be named "Ptarmigan" in honor of the state bird...but the townspeople didn't know how to spell it.

• Towns named for parts of the body, from the head down: Sweet Lips, Tennessee; Left Hand, West Virginia; Shoulderblade, Kentucky; Bowlegs, Oklahoma; and Bigfoot, Texas.

OUTER SPACE

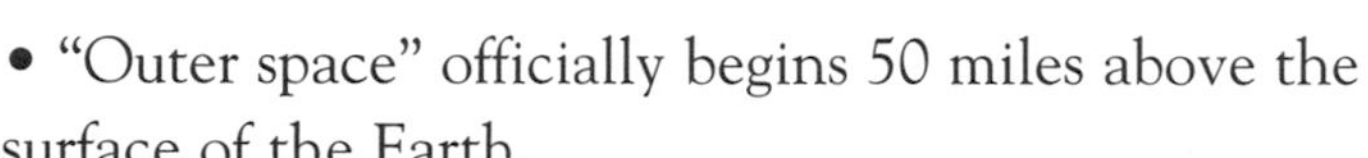

• "Outer space" officially begins 50 miles above the surface of the Earth.

• If you were in a car traveling at 100 miles per hour, it would take you *29 million years* to reach the nearest star.

• You may not be able to feel it, but our galaxy—the Milky Way—revolves a million miles per day, or 40,000 miles per hour.

• If the universe were the size of a building 20 miles long, 20 miles wide, and 20 miles high, all the matter it contains would add up to a single grain of sand.

• What are your chances of being hit by a meteorite? Slim. The mathematical probability is that only one person will get bonked every 180 years.

• Start counting! There are more stars in the universe than there are grains of sand on Earth.

• A comet's tail always points away from the Sun.

• Because of the speed of the Earth's rotation, it's impossible for a solar eclipse to last more than 7 minutes and 58 seconds.

• A *galaxy* is a huge system of stars, typically containing between 10 million and 1 trillion stars each. Our galaxy is called the Milky Way. Astronomers estimate that the universe contains 100 billion galaxies *besides* ours.

AT THE MOVIES

• The first movie theater in the United States was the Vitascope Hall, built in 1896. Where was it? Hollywood? Nope. New Orleans.

• China has about 1,000 movie theaters. That's one movie theater for every million people.

• Almost three billion movie tickets are sold every year in India—an average of three tickets per person. (Americans buy about five tickets per person.)

• The weather is so nice in Greece that many movie theaters don't have roofs.

• John Ratzenberger, the actor who played the mailman Cliff Clavin on *Cheers*, is Pixar's "good-luck charm." Ratzenberger has been in every film Pixar's made. He was the voice of Hamm in *Toy Story*, the Abominable Snowman in *Monsters, Inc.*, P.T. Flea in *A Bug's Life*, a school of fish in *Finding Nemo*, the Underminer in *The Incredibles*, and Mack in *Cars*.

• Some scientists say that *Jurassic Park* portrayed velociraptors inaccurately. In real life, they probably weren't as vicious as they were on-screen.

• Phone numbers used in movies and TV shows always begin with "555." Why? No *real* phone number starts with 555, so viewers can't dial the number from the movie and bother the poor person who happens to have that number.

CONDIMENTS

- What does *salsa* mean? It's Spanish for "sauce."
- Ketchup was once sold as medicine. The miracle sauce was advertised as a cure for all sorts of illnesses and maladies, including baldness and athlete's foot.
- What's the difference between mayonnaise and Miracle Whip? Miracle Whip is mayonnaise with corn syrup and sugar added.
- A1 steak sauce contains raisins.
- The earliest known recipe for mustard appeared in 42 A.D.
- Pour it on: Half a cup of ketchup contains as much nutrition as a large tomato.
- After astronauts complained about the bland food they had to eat during spaceflights, NASA chefs included Tabasco Sauce in the kitchens of the Space Shuttles and the International Space Station.
- The ancient Chinese were the first to make ketchup. Called *kachiap*, it was made with pickled fish and spices—not tomatoes.
- U.S. troops have used miniature Tabasco bottles to make chess sets and Christmas tree decorations.
- Tartar sauce is typically used on fried seafood dishes, but in Seattle, Washington, it's more popular on French fries than ketchup.

PLANET OF THE APES

• A group of citizens in Mesa, Arizona, are circulating a petition against the police department's intention to train a tiny monkey that they can dress in a bulletproof vest and send into dangerous situations.

• Scientists say that young female chimps are smarter than young males.

• A species of monkey recently discovered in Tanzania communicates in honking barks. Scientists think it's different enough to have its own new genus: *Rungwecebus*.

• After a young colobus monkey escaped from Ireland's Belfast Zoo, zookeepers told the press that the monkey had recently had an argument with his dad.

• In 2003 Los Angeles customs officials arrested a man for trying to smuggle two pygmy monkeys into the United States. Where'd he hide them? In his pants.

• Apes have blood types similar to humans, but chimpanzees mostly have blood type A, almost no blood type O, and never blood type B. On the other hand, gorillas have blood type B, almost no blood type O, and never blood type A.

• The Vegetarian Banquet for Monkeys is an annual tradition at a Buddhist shrine in Thailand. The guest list in 2004 included more than 3,000 macaques.

THE END

All Good Things Must Come to an End

• In 2005, the top three deadliest jobs in the United States were logger, airline pilot, and deep-sea fisherman.

• At high levels, carbon monoxide gas can kill a person in under three minutes.

• In Hong Kong, about 12 people are killed every year by trash that's thrown out of windows.

• Smoking is the number-one leading cause of death in the United States. The second leading cause of death? Poor diet.

• Of the 2,245 people onboard the *Titanic*, 1,513 perished and 732 survived.

• Henry Ford owned a bottle containing the last breath of his friend Thomas Edison. It was caught and sealed in the bottle on October 18, 1931.

• Ferocious warrior Attila the Hun died of a nosebleed.

• In 65 B.C., the Greek playwright Aeschylus was killed when an eagle dropped a tortoise on his head.

• The creator of *Star Trek*, Gene Roddenberry, died in 1991. Six years later, a cylinder containing his ashes was shot into outer space.

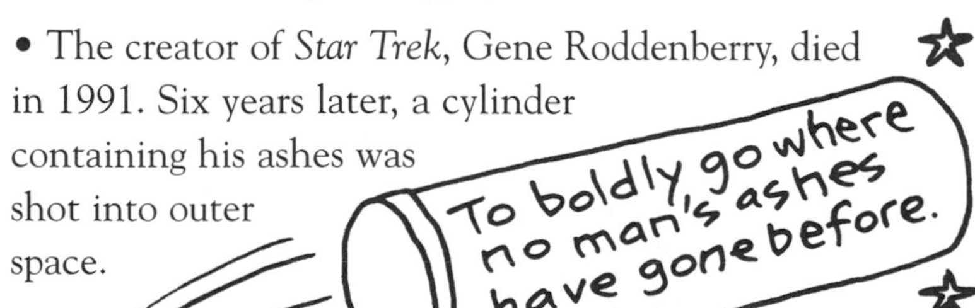

THE MOON

• For every one time the Earth orbits the Sun, the Moon orbits the Earth 13 times.

• The largest known crater in the solar system is on the far side of the Moon (the side facing away from Earth). It is 1,454 miles (2,340 km) across and eight miles (13 km) deep—more than twice as big as Alaska and deeper than the deepest part of the Pacific Ocean.

• The Moon doesn't radiate its own light—when we see moonlight, what we see is actually sunlight reflected off the Moon's surface.

• Light from the Moon gets to Earth in about 1.5 seconds.

• The distance from Earth to the Moon: about 15,654,023,458 inches.

• The Moon is one-fourth the size of the Earth.

• Flying around the Moon's equator, you would cover the same distance as flying from New York to London and back again.

• Full moons occur every 29 or 30 days. A "blue moon" is the second of two full moons that appear in the same calendar month.

• Don't look for a full moon on Halloween: During the past 100 years, it's happened only four times—in 1925, 1944, 1955, and 1974. The next October 31 full moon will be in 2020.

JUNK FOOD

- Twinkies are about 68% air.
- Thinking of entering a doughnut-eating contest? Here's a tip: Press down hard on the doughnut before biting into it, so the air inside doesn't bloat your belly.
- The world's longest hot dog: a 1,996-foot wiener made by Sara Lee Corp. for the 1996 Olympics. Unfortunately, the "Olympic Weenie" wasn't refrigerated, so it couldn't be eaten.
- Krispy Kreme makes about five million doughnuts a day in its North American stores.
- In 1886, its first year in business, Coca-Cola sold an average of nine bottles a day. In 2000, people in more than 200 countries drank nearly 571 million servings of Coca-Cola in just one day.
- Depending on how you measure it, San Francisco's Golden Gate Bridge is 4,200 feet—or 28,800 Oreo cookies—long.
- In 2006 a Coca-Cola employee tried to sell one of Coke's secret recipes to Pepsi…but Pepsi turned him in.
- On July 4, 2006, Takeru Kobayashi won the International Hot Dog Eating Contest for the sixth year in a row. He ate 53¾ hot dogs (with the buns) in just 12 minutes—more than one wiener every 15 seconds.

ANOTHER VISIT TO MICROBIA

• In the world of microbes (microorganisms), the smallest of the small is the *parvovirus*. It's so tiny it can be seen only through a high-power microscope.

• Seaweed and kelp may look a lot like plants, but they actually belong to the same family as microbes.

• Viruses are versatile: They can infect every form of life, including fungi, bacteria, plants, animals…and you.

• If you could stack bacteria, it would take about 500 of them to equal the thickness of one thin dime.

• Fungi are everywhere! They live on your body, in your house, on plants and animals, in the soil, and in fresh and salt water.

• A single teaspoon of topsoil contains about 120,000 fungi.

• Viruses have a unique way of reproducing: invading and taking over other cells (like the ones in your body).

• Each square centimeter of your skin is home to an average of about 100,000 active, healthy bacteria.

• Slime molds normally live as individual cells, but in poor conditions they group together. When they do, look out! They form a slimy, sluglike structure that can crawl off to a new location.

DON'T BE A DAFTY!

If you've run out of names to call your friends, try some of these from Cumbria in northwest England.

- A "gammerstang" is a big girl with bad manners.
- A silly, talkative person is a "bletherskite."
- What's a "mæzlin?" A person with no sense.

- A tattletale is a "clat."
- Someone who's incompetent is "feckless."
- Someone who says flattering things is a "flaach."
- A big bully is a "gomcrel." (Though in other places in England, a gomerel is a fool.)
- "Goamless" is the word for cowardly.
- A blunderer is a "maffelhorn."
- Know anyone who's totally useless? You'd call him a "wæster."
- A rogue or a scamp is a "taggelt."
- A lazy guy who slinks around is a "slonk."
- A woman who's dressed extravagantly is a "flîgæry."
- A "tæstrel" is a violent or mischievous person.
- Lots of words for idiots: Try "dafty," "clot-head," "dummel head," or "gowk."

HERE, DOGGIE

- Dobermans were first bred by Louis Dobermann, a German tax collector who wanted a dog for protection from bandits—*and* for intimidating taxpayers.
- The oldest American breed is the American Foxhound. Hounds came with the first settlers; the American Foxhound developed from those dogs.
- In the United States, an estimated one million dogs have been named in their owners' wills.
- The Saluki, a graceful variety of hound, is represented in Sumerian carvings that date all the way back to 7000 B.C.
- Greyhounds can stride a distance of 27 feet.
- A dog's ear is controlled by 17 muscles.
- True or false: Dalmations are born with all their spots. False! They're born with white coats, and the black spots develop later.
- Chow Chows have tongues and gums that start out pink at birth but turn bluish-black by the time they're eight weeks old.
- Basset Hounds can't swim. Their legs are too short to keep their long, heavy bodies afloat.
- Who's Bingo? (He's the dog on the Cracker Jack box.)

WORD ORIGINS

You've heard them here and there, but where do they come from?

• The word "worm" is from *wyrm*, the Old English word for dragon. In ancient times, worms and insects were classified with serpents.

• Bungalow, pajamas, jungle, and shampoo are all from the Hindi language.

• The term "devil's advocate" comes from the Roman Catholic Church. A devil's advocate argues the case against appointing someone a saint.

• "Mayday" comes from the French *m'aider*, a shortening of *venez m'aider*: "Come help me!"

• If you ice skate, you probably know what a Zamboni is. The machine used in ice rinks to smooth the ice is named for its inventor, Frank Zamboni, who created the first one from a tractor.

• The abbreviation for pound—lb.—comes from the Latin *libra*, the word for scale. People in the Middle Ages did their weighing and accounting in Latin.

• "Chameleon" is from the Greek word for "little lion."

• The word "moose" comes from the Algonquian Indian word meaning "twig eater."

IN LIVING COLOR

- Technically, black and white are not colors. White contains *all* the colors of the visible spectrum and black is the *absence* of color.
- In 10th-century France, the doors of traitors and criminals were painted yellow.
- The color yellow has come to mean "cowardly." It used to be common to say a cowardly person had a "yellow streak" or was "yellow-bellied."
- Greenish blue is called *turquoise*; bluish green is called *teal.*
- The ancient Persians believed all gods wore white.
- In ancient Rome, public servants wore blue. Interestingly, even today, many police officers and other public servants wear blue uniforms.
- At Easter in Greece, eggs are dyed red for good luck.
- Red means good luck in China, too. It's used especially for holidays and weddings.
- Ancient Egyptians colored the floors of their temples green.
- Leonardo da Vinci believed that the power of meditation increased by 10 times when it was performed in purple light, for instance in the purple light of stained glass.

COMMERCIAL CHARACTERS

• Tony the Tiger, the Frosted Flakes mascot, is married and has a son and a daughter. His wife's name: Mama Tiger. His children are Tony Jr. and Antoinette.

• A male actor provided the voice of the famous Taco Bell Chihuahua, but the dog you saw in the commercials was a girl dog named Gidget.

• The Energizer Bunny has made cameo appearances in commercials for Purina Cat Chow and Hostess Twinkies.

• The oldest and most enduring cartoon characters to advertise a Kellogg's product are Snap! Crackle! and Pop! of Rice Krispies fame.

• When the Jolly Green Giant first appeared in 1928, he wasn't jolly at all. He was a scowling, hunchbacked giant in a scruffy old bearskin.

• Back in the 1930s, Pepsi had an advertising campaign starring two cartoon cops named "Pepsi & Pete."

• Ronald McDonald's face is recognized by more than 95% of American children.

• A Pillsbury Doughboy doll released in 1972 was so popular that *Playthings* magazine named it Toy of the Year.

PANGRAMS

A pangram is a sentence containing all 26 letters of the alphabet, like the classic "The quick brown fox jumps over the lazy dog." But there are lots more where that came from.

- A mad boxer shot a quick, gloved jab to the jaw of his dizzy opponent.
- About sixty codfish eggs will make a quarter pound of very fizzy jelly.
- Amazingly few discotheques provide jukeboxes.
- By Jove, my quick study of lexicography won a prize.

- Crazy Fredericka bought many very exquisite opal jewels.
- Jaded zombies acted quaintly but kept driving their oxen forward.
- Exquisite farm wench gives body jolt to prize stinker.
- Uncle John's fake, girly Pez-box liquid washed MTV.
- Grumpy wizards make toxic brew for the evil queen and jack.
- Jolly housewives made inexpensive meals using quick-frozen vegetables.
- The xylophone orchestra vowed to imbibe jugs of kumquat fizz.

THE POOP ON PIGS

• According to scientists, pigs are the smartest domesticated animals.

• Why do pigs roll around in the mud? They can't sweat, so they coat themselves in mud to cool off.

• The pygmy hog of India—the world's smallest pig—weighs about 10 pounds.

• In the 1860s, about 10,000 wild pigs roamed New York City. They ate garbage.

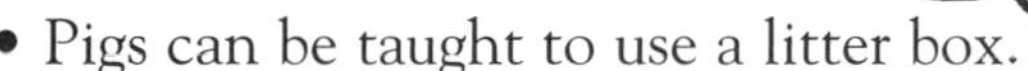

• Pigs can be taught to use a litter box.

• Pigs were first domesticated over 7,000 years ago.

• Ben & Jerry's sends ice cream waste to local pig farms near its Vermont headquarters. The pigs love it all...except for Mint Chocolate Cookie.

• Engineers in Finland used pig poop to clean a contaminated pond near an old mine. The bacteria in the poop attracted the metals that polluted the water, and the combination sank to the bottom.

• In 2006, 12 piglets from seven countries took part in the Pig Olympics in Moscow, competing in pig-racing, pig-swimming, and pigball, a piggy version of soccer.

IT'S A WILD WORLD

• Of the approximately 4,680 species of mammals, nearly half are rodents, and about one-fifth are bats.

• Biggest clam: the tridacna. It can grow four feet wide and weigh up to 500 pounds.

• All animals with hooves are close relatives of whales and dolphins—the rhino seems to be the closest.

• Male Dayak fruit bats are the only male mammals known to produce milk—and they suckle their young just like the females do.

• There's a deer in Asia called a "mouse deer." The little guy is only nine inches tall.

• A pregnant polar bear can live off her stored fat for up to eight months while traveling hundreds of miles to give birth and nursing her cubs until they're more than 10 times their birth weight.

• Hyenas are closely related to cats, but hunt like dogs.

• You probably know that camels can go a long time—up to several months—without drinking. They can also down 13 gallons of water in just a few minutes.

• B-r-r. Z-z-z. B-r-r. Z-z-z. Many species of bats can survive freezing temperatures when they hibernate.

BUILDING BLOCKS

What puts the "you" in human…

• You genes, called the "blueprints of life," determine almost everything about you, from your eye color to your shoe size. They tell your cells how to make muscles, nerves, bones—and every other part.

• Cell Fact #1: A cell is the smallest unit of matter considered to be alive.

• Cell Fact #2: There are about 200 different kinds of cells in your body, each with a unique shape and a unique job to do.

• In the center of every cell is a *nucleus*. In the nucleus are several pairs of chromosomes. Chromosomes are crucial because they carry your genes.

• Humans have 23 pairs of chromosomes in each cell. Mosquitoes have 3 pairs, goldfish have 52 pairs, and onions have 8 pairs.

• Cell Fact #3: Every individual cell in your body is a living creature. If you put a single skin cell in a dish with nutrients, it would continue to live—and even crawl around!

FOOD, GLORIOUS FOOD

• Should we check the expiration date? Graham crackers, Jell-O, instant coffee, Triscuit crackers, Campbell's Tomato Soup, and Fig Newtons have all been around for more than 100 years.

• When a swarm of locusts landed on Beijing, China, in 2002, they were scooped up, deep fried…and eaten.

• In 1895, C.W. Post created the very first grocery coupon by offering shoppers 1¢ off the purchase of the company's new health cereal, Grape-Nuts.

• Americans eat approximately 100 acres of pizza a day. That's an average of 350 slices per second.

• Sometimes when you want to sell something, you have to give it away—that's what Kellogg's did in 1907 when it introduced its new breakfast food. They gave away a free box of Kellogg's Corn Flakes to every woman who winked at the grocer.

• In 2000, the H. J. Heinz, Co. experienced its biggest spike in sales since the company was founded in 1869. That's when they introduced green ketchup.

• Some people believe tea originated in China on a very windy day. According to legend, a strong wind blew tea leaves into a pot of boiling water.

• Biggest cereal maker in the world: Quaker Oats.

• The most popular pizza toppings in India: dill, ginger, and lamb.

• What do you call a plain, unsalted pretzel? A "baldy."

• Three jars of peanut butter are sold every second.

• Americans eat nearly 20 billion pickles per year. That's more than nine pounds per person a year.

• Almost everybody (98%) spreads the peanut butter on first when they're making a peanut butter and jelly sandwich.

• The average American eats 24 pounds of cheese per year. That's nothing compared to the French: They eat 43.6 pounds of cheese per person, per year.

• Don't try this at home: Among nuts, macadamias have the hardest shells in the world. It takes approximately 300 pounds of pressure to open them.

• There are at least 1,462 edible insect species in the world. The most popular way to prepare an insect is to cook it live, like a crab or a lobster, and then peel it open and eat the insides.

• Eight out of 10 American families have a box of oatmeal in the kitchen cupboard.

• In Japan, you can taste some unusual ice cream flavors, including horseradish, crab, squid ink, buttered potato, ox tongue, cactus, and chicken wing.

BOOKS

• According to one theory, the word "book" comes from *bok*, meaning "beech" in Old English, because the first books in Europe were written on slabs of beechwood.

• The British Library owns the world's oldest existing printed book: a Buddhist text called *Diamond Sutra*, published in China in 868 A.D.

• A book of maps is called an *atlas* because the covers of early editions featured pictures of the mythical Greek character Atlas carrying the world on his shoulders.

• The Bible is the bestselling book of all time. More than six billion copies have been sold.

• *The Da Vinci Code* is the bestselling adult novel of all time within a *one-year period*: 6.8 million copies.

• *Orbis Pictus (The Visible World in Pictures)*, a children's encyclopedia, was published in 1658 by a Czech educator. It's considered to be the very first picture book for children.

• A *bibliophile* is a person who loves books.

• Ms. Kazuko Hosoki from Japan has written a series of 81 books on fortune telling, with a total of 34,000,000 copies sold.

• An 1859 first edition of Darwin's *On the Origin of Species by Means of Natural Selection* was returned to a Boston public library in 2001—80 years overdue.

SHARK ATTACK!

- There are about 375 species of shark.
- Great whites are the sharks most commonly responsible for attacks on people. They have a very good sense of smell. How good? They can smell a single drop of blood in an Olympic-size swimming pool.
- Shark attacks are very rare. You have better odds of winning the lottery than being attacked by a shark.
- Some sharks, like blacktip reef sharks, hunt in groups. Blacktip reef sharks can also jump all the way out of the water or just stick their noses out of the water to look around. (Look out, seagulls!)
- Sharks have the unusual ability to sense minute electrical fields that are generated by other creatures. This sixth sense is possible because of specialized sensory organs called the *ampullae of Lorenzini*.
- Great white, tiger, hammerhead, and bull sharks are known as apex predators—they have no natural enemies.
- Scientific research suggests that sharks are the only animals that never get sick. They appear to be immune to every known disease, including cancer.
- The largest shark in the world is the docile whale shark. It can grow to 80 feet long.
- Over its lifetime, a shark can lose and regrow more than 20,000 teeth.

• The cookie-cutter shark is less than two feet long.

• An extinct species of shark, the megalodon shark, was the biggest in the history of the world—so big that it could eat a Tyrannosaurus rex.

• Another extinct species is the iniopterygians shark. It had winglike fins that enabled it to fly short distances.

• During World War II, some fighter planes used shark oil to lubricate instruments.

• The fastest sharks in the sea, mako sharks can swim up to 20 mph.

• Hammerhead sharks have the weirdest looking heads of all sharks: a thick, flat head with eyes on the outside that looks…like the head of a hammer.

• Lantern sharks glow in the dark. Tiny, too: Some grow only to 10 inches long.

• A basking shark has 3,000 teeth.

• The zebra shark's skin is unique. When they're young, they have stripes, but as they grow older, the stripes turn into dots.

• Megamouth sharks were only discovered in 1976, and only 36 have ever been sighted. Their immense mouths are 40 inches wide.

• The fin that sticks out of the water is called the dorsal fin.

• A shark's ears are on the inside of its head.

I DO! I DO!

• It takes about 9½ months to plan the average American wedding.

• The tradition of wearing the wedding ring on the third finger of the left hand began in ancient Rome. The Romans believed that the vein that runs through that finger is connected directly to the heart.

• In the United States, June is the most popular month for weddings. On the other hand, most couples in the Philippines get married in December.

• Ancient Romans used to throw cakes at the wedding couple to symbolically bless the marriage with abundance and fertility.

• For good luck, German brides used to carry salt and bread in their pocket. Grooms carried grain.

• Two hundred people are invited to the average wedding. (But they don't all attend.)

• In the 17th and 18th centuries, pies were a part of a marriage celebration. The "bride's pie" was filled with mincemeat or mutton. A glass ring was hidden deep inside the pie. The woman who wound up with the piece of pie with the ring in it was said to be the next to marry.

MAKES CENTS

• The old Spanish peso was sometimes cut into bits to make change. That's where the terms "pieces of eight" and "two bits" come from.

• The largest bank in the United States, the Bank of America, was originally called the Bank of Italy.

• Coin collectors are called *numismatists*. But they don't just collect coins—they collect medals, paper money, and tokens, too.

• When the French first settled Quebec in 1685, they sent troops to keep law and order, but forgot to send money to pay them. Instead, they paid the troops with playing cards. Even when real money finally arrived from France, the troops liked the card money so much that they continued to use it for another 30 years.

• The life expectancy of paper money is only about 18 months. Coins can stay in circulation for 30 years.

• The difference between the face value of a coin and the value of the metal in it is called *seigniorage*.

• Two nicknames for silver dollars: the Ferris wheel and the cartwheel.

• One billion dollars in $1 bills weighs a little more than 2,048 pounds. A billion dollars in $100 bills weighs just 20.4 pounds.

GOT MILK?

• A process known as "pasteurization" is used to kill all the *pathogens* (disease-causing bacteria) in milk. The milk is heated to at least 161°F for about 15 seconds and then rapidly cooled.

• Some harmless bacteria survive the pasteurization process, which is why you still need to refrigerate milk.

• When Louis Pasteur, the man who developed the pasteurization process, discovered those invisible germs, he became obsessed with cleanliness. He washed and rewashed his hands all day—and when he was done he washed the soap!

• Grade A milk—even if it's pasteurized—can have almost five million germs per 8-ounce glass.

• Ever been pouring milk when a big goober of cream plopped on top of your cereal? Buy *homogenized* milk the next time. It's been sprayed through a small hole at high pressure, a process that chops the butterfat globules so tiny they can't clump together anymore.

• The first "Got Milk?" TV ad was "Aaron Burr"—or "Awooon Buuuh," as pronounced by the peanut-butter-eating history buff who was trying to answer a radio quiz question. In the 10+ years since then, the California Milk Processor Board has used the "Got Milk?" gimmick in over 60 commercials.

SOUVENIR SHOP

• In the 1800s, Iroquois began selling souvenirs to tourists at Niagara Falls.

• In 1846, Philadelphia city officials chipped off tiny pieces of the Liberty Bell to give as souvenirs to visiting dignitaries.

• The first snow globe, made in France in the late 1880s, contained a tiny Eiffel Tower.

• The gladiator games of ancient Rome drew such large crowds that street vendors sold all sorts of cheesy souvenirs—even pots of sweat from gladiator superstars. (Ewww!)

• In the early 1900s, reports of the shrunken heads made by the native tribes of Ecuador started a frenzy for the odd souvenirs among well-to-do Europeans. While there were collectors who really lost their heads searching for shrunken heads, most tourists unwittingly returned with fakes made from goatskin.

• Astronaut James Irwin had to leave his jacket on the Moon to lighten the spacecraft for the trip home, but he cut out his NASA name tag to bring home. The moon dust-covered souvenir sold at auction for $310,500.

• In the first year after its demolition, 59 tons of rubble from the Berlin Wall were shipped to the United States and sold as souvenirs.

SILLY WORLD RECORDS

• In 1998, John Evans of Sheffield, England earned the world record for book balancing. He balanced a column of 62 identical books on his head that weighed 217 pounds and measured over six feet tall.

• The world record for standing on one leg: 71 hours.

• Go, Granny, go! The official world record for rocking in a rocking chair is 480 hours.

• In 1991, Pringles baked the largest potato chip on record. The monster chip contained 920 calories and measured 23 inches by 14.5 inches.

• Britain's Scott Day spun a coin for 19.37 seconds.

• In April 1992, the staff at Cadbury Red Tulip of Australia made the world's largest chocolate Easter egg—it weighed 10,482 pounds, 14 ounces.

• Weighing in at more than 3,000 pounds, the largest serving of guacamole was made during the Fiesta con Sabor a Mexico at the Latino Cultural Center in Dallas, Texas, in 2005.

• The smallest kite ever flown—smaller than one inch square—was designed and built by a member of the International Friends of Small Kites organization.

THE BETTER TO BITE YOU WITH

• An alligator has about 80 teeth. As they wear down, new ones grow in to replace them.

• Goats have no upper front teeth.

• Ancient Mexicans wore dentures made from wolves' teeth—for decorative purposes only.

• Watch out! Some police departments replace their police dogs' teeth with teeth made of titanium.

• The longest teeth in the world are elephant tusks.

• The Etruscans invented false teeth about 2,700 years ago.Their version was made of bone and ivory, and laced together by gold bands.

• Giraffes have just as many teeth as humans: 32.

• A New Orleans dentist invented modern dental floss—a piece of silk thread—in 1815.

• Where are your eyeteeth? They're the two upper canines—the pointy teeth under your eyes.

• A male babirusa pig's teeth are deadly…to itself. The upper canines develop into tusks that grow through the snout and curve back toward the eyes. Eventually they will pierce the skull, killing the animal.

• Some dolphins have over 200 teeth, making it the mammal with the most teeth in the world.

SMART REMARKS

"Any smoothly functioning technology gives the appearance of magic." —**Arthur C. Clarke**

"I am always doing that which I cannot do, in order that I may learn how to do it." —**Pablo Picasso**

"The future is something which everyone reaches at the rate of 60 minutes an hour, whatever he does, whoever he is." —**C. S. Lewis**

"A little nonsense now and then is relished by the wisest men." —**Roald Dahl**

"The most wasted of all days is one without laughter." —**e. e. cummings**

"What you give comes back to you." —**Oprah Winfrey**

"It is our choices that show what we truly are, far more than our abilities." —**Albus Dumbledore,** ***Harry Potter and the Chamber of Secrets***

"Do not go where the path may lead. Go instead where there is no path…and leave a trail." —**Ralph Waldo Emerson**

"Just play. Have fun. Enjoy the game." —**Michael Jordan**

Come on...
TAKE THE PLUNGE!

To read a few sample chapters, go to our website and visit the "Throne Room" at
www.bathroomreader.com

Also available from the BRI:
An ever-growing assortment of great gift ideas:

T-shirts
Calendars
Mini Books
Tote Bags
Bumper Stickers
Toilet Paper
...and more!

Uncle John's Bathroom Readers FOR KIDS ONLY!

THE LAST PAGE

FELLOW BATHROOM READERS: Bathroom reading should never be taken loosely, so Sit Down and Be Counted! Join the Bathroom Readers' Institute. Just go to *www.bathroomreader.com* to sign up. It's free! Or send a self-addressed, stamped envelope and your email address to: Bathroom Readers' Institute, P.O. Box 1117, Ashland, Oregon 97520. You'll receive a free membership card, our BRI newsletter (sent out via e-mail), discounts when ordering directly through the BRI, and you'll earn a permanent spot on the BRI honor roll!

UNCLE JOHN'S NEXT
BATHROOM READER FOR KIDS ONLY
IS ALREADY IN THE WORKS!

Is there a subject you'd like to read about in our next *Uncle John's Bathroom Reader* for kids? Write to us at *www.bathroomreader.com* and let us know. We aim to please.

Well, we're out of space, and when you've got to go, you've got to go. Hope to hear from you soon. Meanwhile, remember...

Go with the Flow!